HOW TO BE A

GREAT
PARENT

DR. NANCY S. BUCK

HOW TO BE A
GREAT
PARENT

Understanding
Your Child's
Wants and Needs

Library of Congress Cataloging-in-Publication Data Buck, Nancy S. How to be a great parent : understanding your child's wants and needs / Nancy S. Buck.   p. cm. Includes index. ISBN 978-0-8253-0689-1 (pbk. : alk. paper) -- ISBN 978-0-8253-0650-1 (ebook) 1. Parenting. 2. Parent and child. I. Title. HQ755.8.B82 2013 649'.1--dc23 2012033250

For inquiries about volume orders, please contact:
Beaufort Books
27 West 20th Street, Suite 1102
New York, NY 10011
sales@beaufortbooks.com

Published in the United States by Beaufort Books
www.beaufortbooks.com

Distributed by Midpoint Trade Books
www.midpointtrade.com

Printed in the United States of America

Interior design by Jane Perini
Cover Design by Tobias Design
Index by Songbird Indexing Services

This book is dedicated to children and parents:
May your lives be filled with peace, joy, and laughter
as you love and grow together.

Contents

 # Introduction

W hat a wonderful and daunting task it is to be a parent! It is the most important job of our lives, yet one for which we are untrained and unprepared. How we parent today will change the future. Even though we can become paralyzed with this realization, once we have taken on this job, we want to do it well.

Where do we get our training for being good, responsible, and loving parents? How do we learn what is necessary to accomplish the most important work we will ever do? Most of us have only our own childhood experiences to help guide and inform our parenting practices. Our most influential teachers are our own parents.

Maybe your parents were good models and teachers, or maybe you never want to be the kind of parent to your own children that your parents were to you. Unfortunately, if you don't have other ideas or models to follow, you may find that you fall back on the parenting practices of your parents, doing exactly what you vowed you would never do.

It's easy to be the kind of parent you want to be when your children are safely tucked into bed at night. During these moments of reflection, you may discover the clarity you were searching for earlier in the day when confronted by your child. Suddenly, you know what you could have said in order to be the kind of parent you imagine being. Where were these brilliant ideas at the moment you needed them most?

During the moments when your child is doing precisely what you want her to do, or wants what you want him to want, parenting is joyous and easy. The hard times are when your darlings start behaving contrary to how you want them to or demand something that you don't want them to have. That's when parenting gets really rough. The true test of how you measure up as a parent comes with how you handle yourself and maintain a loving relationship with your children when your desires, expectations, and interests are in conflict with theirs.

How to Be a Great Parent is written to advise, guide, and direct you during those moments when you wish you knew a better way. It will also help you generate more moments when you and your child are in harmony with each other. Your happy, joyous moments will increase. The difficult, challenging times will still exist, but you will have a better idea how to handle them, and they will decrease in frequency.

I'm recommending a lifelong process rather than a cookbook solution. I recommend these ideas to help you and your child learn how to meet your inherent needs: for love and belonging, for power, for fun, for freedom, and for survival. Understanding what motivates all behavior (yours and your child's) engenders a process that will help and support you as you strive to raise loving, respectful, and responsible children.

● What's in this book

This book explains how to apply choice theory, which is an explanation of human behavior and motivation, to parenting. Each chapter explains how a particular aspect of the theory applies specifically to parenting. To help you understand and apply these new ideas, you'll find some special sections, including easy and fun quizzes, parenting tips, and question-and-answer sections.

Chapter 1 is the most concentrated theory section. Here you will learn why your present method of parenting is less than successful. Like most people, you have probably been applying "common knowledge," an accepted but unsuccessful theory of behavior that is applied to parenting. This chapter will introduce you to new and better science. With this guidance you will be able to understand and apply a new and peaceful parenting process.

Chapter 2 more fully explains choice theory. This chapter will help you understand your children and yourself and offers a new, effective method to help both you and your children. After reading this chapter you will have a new, kinder, more effective, and successful process for dealing with your children's misbehaviors. You will also be able to begin to apply these new techniques immediately!

Chapter 3 helps you plan a peaceful parenting process for coping with your children's repeated misbehaviors. This chapter will give you new, more effective strategies you can immediately apply to these situations instead of hoping for the best, wishing that time alone would change the upsets and hassles in your home, or using the same old ineffective methods of labeling your child as the cause of the repeated upsets.

Chapter 4 will help you refine your new strategies as well as help you define more clearly your new goals for using your new parenting process.

Chapters 5, 6, and 7 will give you more specific methods for dealing with your children's needs for fun, power, and freedom. Along the way you will also increase your ability to meet your own needs for fun, power, and freedom.

Chapters 8, 9, and 10 address specific parenting issues that seem to arise in almost every family. These issues are bedtime, sibling relationships, and teenage rebellion. Chapter 11 offers specific advice for divorced parents who are parenting together even though they are no longer together as a couple.

You may want to go directly to the epilogue. This tells you the absolute, full-proof, no-fail method for successful parenting that every parent can begin applying immediately!

● How to get the most from this book

As you read each section and each chapter, immediately begin to apply the new ideas offered. You could wait until you have read the whole book, go back and reread it, and then apply these new ideas, but I suggest the first method because you will begin experiencing immediate success that will help inspire you to keep going. Either way, however, you'll get the most from this book if you take an idea, put it into action, practice it, and then take the next idea, put it into action, and practice it. Like anything new, the more you practice, the better you will get at applying these new ideas. If you practice enough, this peaceful process will become second nature, a process you can use automatically without having to think, plan, and evaluate continually.

The earlier in your children's lives you start, the longer you will be able to enjoy the benefits of this parenting process. But if your children are teenagers, it is not too late to begin. Even if your children are already adults, it is not too late.

The biggest key to success is to practice, evaluate, adjust, and practice. Don't simply practice, practice, and practice some more. Take the time to evaluate and adjust before you practice more. This reflection time enables you to see what is wrong and what needs refinement and improvement.

Finally, be kind, gentle, and loving with yourself as you courageously attempt an unfamiliar parenting process. The job of parenting is vitally important and incredibly difficult. Luckily, it is also unimaginably rewarding. You are taking the hero's and heroine's journey of learning and applying new strategies. Good for you. Good for your children. And ultimately, it's good for the world.

1.

You can control your child's behavior

And other parenting myths

H elp!" wrote one mother. "My husband says he wants to handle conflicts with our children differently from how he was parented, but he doesn't. For instance, he yells at our four-year-old daughter and six-year-old son when they don't listen to him. He says they are being disrespectful. I say they are being children." Usually, when a parent says that the children "don't listen," what he really means is that the children don't comply with his requests. They may listen when he says, "Go to bed," but then they continue to play or begin to protest. The children have listened; they just haven't complied.

● Why won't my children do what I want them to?

The predominant model for rearing children in most places around the world is based on the idea that adults need to teach, convince, and control children to make them behave as the adults think children should. Like this father, most parents believe children should meet their expectations. When a child misbehaves, most parents attempt to externally control the child through demands ("Knock it off!"), threats ("If you don't behave yourself in this store, you won't get the treat we talked about"), punishment ("You can't watch television tonight because you didn't eat all of your dinner"), or any combination of these means.

Most people believe that they can change other people's behavior if they somehow coerce or externally threaten, punish, or hurt, all in an attempt to control the other person. Often the people parents are trying to control are their children.

Parents also try positive incentives to externally control children. "If you study really hard and get an A on your spelling test, you will have a special treat after dinner." Or, "Because you have done such a wonderful job cooperating with me today, we'll go for an ice cream treat." Coercion through rewards can be just as manipulative and damaging as coercion through threats or punishment. (For a complete understanding of this idea, see Alfie Kohn's book *Punished by Rewards*.) Most adults believe that all people—but especially children—are controllable through external methods. (For further discussion read "Rewarding May Be Counterproductive" in appendix B.)

Would you be surprised to learn that this commonly held belief is wrong? Children cannot be manipulated into behaving just as we want them to. Unfortunately, a great deal of information in our culture leads parents to believe that they can, should, and must control their children.

The reality is that people are not easily controlled. In fact, trying to control other people may make them resist even harder because they do not want to feel dominated. If people were so easy to manipulate, you too would be easily controlled and manipulated.

For instance, can you resist buying everything that is advertised by the media? Of course you can. Even the "bribes" and positive reinforcements the advertisers offer, such as rebates and sale prices, do not induce you to purchase everything willy-nilly. You decide to purchase something because you need or want a specific item, not because of the enticement of advertising.

Do you have the ability to resist your child's unhealthy or inappropriate requests? Of course you do. Even when your child punishes you by telling you she hates you or threatens you, saying she won't love you anymore if you don't give in, you still have the strength to answer your child's request with a firm no. No matter how hard your child tries to externally control you, you can make a reasonable decision and stick to it.

Why do we think it is otherwise with children? Simply because children are smaller, less experienced, and younger than adults does not mean they are any more easily controlled or manipulated by external rewards and punishment. They respond the same way adults do to this type of situation.

You probably have had a personal experience with someone who attempted to control you by using negative or positive coercion. Perhaps you even obeyed and complied. But how would you describe your relationship with this person? Is this someone you feel close to? Is this someone you want to spend time with? Or is this someone you simply tolerate?

Given that we know how unsatisfying this type of relationship is, why do we even consider using this kind of model for raising our children? The goal of every parent I have ever talked with is the same. We want our children to mature into healthy, responsible adults who like us well enough to visit occasionally. However, when we insist on using the predominant model of externally controlling our children, we run the risk that our children will move as far away from us as possible, as fast as they can. This is the opposite of what we want.

Why do parents persist in following this mistaken belief in child rearing? There are two reasons:

- No other model is available.
- Parents are frightened.

How to Be a Great Parent offers parents a different model. Please note: this is not perfect or permissive or easy parenting. But it is a model that teaches parents how to help children mature into responsible and functioning adults who get along without us in the world. It also fosters good relationships with our children throughout their childhoods and beyond.

● Bad psychology

Twelve-year-old Amy is her mother's perfect child. She cares about neatness and being responsible. Being her parent is easy. But her ten-year-old sister, Rebecca, is her mother's challenge. Her mother describes her as chaotic, irresponsible, messy, and forgetful. Her mother tries to help her by making lists and insisting on helping Rebecca empty her school backpack, but nothing she does changes Rebecca's behavior, because Rebecca does not feel helped. Instead, she feels like she is being criticized and bossed around.

Although Mom is full of good intentions, her attempts to help and change Rebecca are based on conventional wisdom, an approach that often does more harm than good.

Did you know that too much of today's conventional wisdom about

parenting tip

Tell your children every day that you love them. Remind them every day how wonderful they are. Reassure your children every day that your life is better because they are in it. You never know what might happen, so be sure to tell them you love them every day.

behavior and motivation is based on old psychologies? These old psychological theories have made their way into our everyday and casual consciousness, but they are neither sound nor accurate.

These old ideas can be traced back to two sources: Sigmund Freud and behaviorism doctrine. Sigmund Freud was a groundbreaking psychiatrist who changed the world's understanding of mental illness. Prior to Freud's contributions to psychology, a person who was mentally ill was not considered to be ill at all but instead to be possessed by the devil. Freud, a physician, suggested that people's upsets were illnesses, like measles. This is how the world thinks about mental illness today.

In addition, Freud put forth a theory about our personalities and psychic energies. He suggested that we are all driven by the libido, the driving force for life. Many people now interpret this idea narrowly, thinking that the libido represents our sexual desire. For Freud, however, sexual desire was only part of the libido. Libido is our life force, driving us and causing us to strive toward pleasure and survival.

Freud then described the three parts of the psyche: the id, the ego, and the superego. The id represents a child, driven by untamed instinct and continually seeking physical pleasure and fulfillment of desire. The superego represents the authoritative parent who is trying to tame the unruly id. The superego is driven by propriety, decorum, morals, mores, and rules, and it strives for structure and regulation. In the middle is the ego, the part of our psyche that tries to balance and regulate the two extremes of the id and the superego.

The point of this psychology lesson is that many people still believe that a child is as Freud described the id: a wild and unruly mass of animal instincts. Left untended, they believe, children will follow their nature, always doing what makes them feel good. How many times have you heard that children have difficulty accepting delayed gratification? In other words, children are too immature to delay receiving immediate pleasure at any cost.

All of these ideas are the legacy of Sigmund Freud. He was certainly a remarkable and courageous man, who changed the world's view of psychology, behavior, and motivation. However, just because these ideas are more widely known and understood does not make them effective models for parenting.

Behaviorism is another school of thought in psychology that has really taken hold today, with its roots going back to the 1950s. Understanding the motivation for the inception of this school of psychological theory is especially important.

Many in the academic community considered psychology to be a "soft" science because no good research substantiated its ideas. For example, no research had been done to prove the existence of an id, ego, and superego. (This is still true today.) Also, no research proved a correlation between adolescents' sexual development and when they were toilet trained or whether they were bottle- or breast-fed. Although these psychological ideas existed, no research backed up these claims.

Because they wanted psychology to meet the criteria for a "hard" science, behaviorists began conducting research so they could demonstrate cause and effect. That meant they could only study the *demonstrated behavior* of humans (and most often rats). The thoughts of a nine-year-old could not be observed or measured. But the number of times a rat pushed a lever to receive food could be counted. Thus behaviorism was a science that was developed *to meet the criteria of science.* If hard science accepted only that which could be proved through cause-and-effect experimentation and psychology wanted to be a hard science, then cause-and-effect experimentation had to be used. Behaviorism theory was the only psychological theory that met the criteria for hard science. It was developed to meet the specific hard-science criteria of cause-and-effect experimentation. However, it does not mean that other psychological theories are any less legitimate.

Behaviorism tells us that we can control other people's behavior by offering rewards to elicit the behavior we want to encourage and punishments or threats of harm to discourage the behavior we want to eliminate. Experiments with rats have proven this theory, so it must be true. Although this idea may seem like common sense, you have probably had experiences that led you to doubt this scientific theory.

For example, according to behaviorism, once you have received a speeding ticket, you will never speed again because you want to avoid this negative consequence. After receiving a ticket, you probably did stop speeding for a time. The amount of time varies from person to person, but every person who has ever received a speeding ticket has not stopped speeding altogether. Why? Because people don't wake up one morning and say to themselves, "Today I think I will break the law. I wonder how? I know, I think I'll exceed the lawful speed limit."

The reason we speed is not to satisfy our desire to go faster or break the law. The reason we speed is that we want to get someplace in less time.

Imposing a negative external consequence does not alter the behavior. At best, it results in compliance. But more often, a negative consequence or the threat of one will result in the exact opposite of the behavior we hope for. Not only do we not get compliance, we too often get defiance.

Of course, all parents have times when a little compliance seems like a great idea. And occasionally you can ask your child to "please just go along with me this time," even though he thinks your ideas are silly and your request unjust. In fact, asking for compliance occasionally will actually work better than demanding, threatening, or trying to coerce your child to obey.

Those times when you receive a little cooperation and compliance will happen much more frequently if you do not coerce or attempt to externally manipulate behavior using threats or punishment. Is that a scenario that you are interested in?

● New and better science to the rescue

By now you no doubt realize that the faulty parenting methods we use stem from the bad psychology that permeates our culture. You are not a bad parent. If you don't *know* any better, how can you possibly *do* any better? My hope is that this book will give you lots of new and better ideas to help you become a more effective and satisfied parent.

Science that is just emerging has not yet become part of the conventional wisdom of our culture. Once you begin to understand this new science, you will be able to change your parenting style. We will begin with two very specific ideas that will certainly help.

First, Bruce Lipton, Ph.D., has written a book with information that dramatically changes our basic understanding of cellular biology. As Lipton researched the cloning of human muscle tissue, he discovered two astounding facts about cells. Lipton says that human beings are a community of cooperative cells. If you understand how a single cell

Your four-year-old daughter spilled her milk (again) at the dinner table. Which of the following statements do you think would best foster your child's growth and learning?

- "Let's get a sponge and clean this mess up together."
- "I'll get the sponge. You get your Minnie Mouse cup with the top and the straw to fill up with more milk."
- "Move away from the table so that milk doesn't spill on your new dress."

Obviously your tone of voice and your level of stress will affect any one of these responses. You also need to be sure that your frame of mind is such that you are open to your own growth if you are going to foster your child's growth. Can you see that one of these answers would be better than the others to keep your daughter feeling safe enough to learn from this mistake?

works, then you understand how the community of cooperative cells (also known as a human being) works. Cancer cells, in his view, are cells that are not willing to cooperate with the community. This means that the idea of "the survival of the fittest" is only part of the truth about who we are as humans. In fact, cooperation plays a larger role in our lives than competition.

The second important, simple, and powerful idea that Lipton explains is that a cell can be in only one of two positions. A cell is not ever in a neutral position; it is in the position of either protection or growth. Since people are a community of cooperative cells, people operate as the cell. We too are in a position of protection or growth. This means we cannot grow and learn if we are frightened, anxious, or worried. Fear, anxiety, and worry place us in a position of protection. We can only grow and learn when we feel safe, protected, and free to experiment and fail without negative consequences.

Once we internalize this information, our job as parents becomes clearer. If we want our children to grow, thrive, learn, and create to blossom into the best people they can possibly be, then we must create an environment of protection, safety, and security. But if we follow the old model and threaten our children with negative consequences for misbehavior, are we creating an environment that fosters protection or growth? What kind of environment are we creating if we rush our children, telling them to hurry up or we will be late?

How do you handle an incident when your child makes a mistake? What if this is a mistake your child has already made more than a few times? *Does your reaction foster your child's growth or does it cause your child to seek protection from you?* Armed with this question, you can profoundly change your approach to parenting. Not only can you foster your child's growth, you can also foster your own!

This new science also reveals another idea that can help us understand our children and ourselves. Our brains are set up as a negative feedback loop. This means that the difference between what we want and what we perceive as our reality is what generates behavior. This revolutionary idea does not come from psychology but rather comes from engineering as well as cellular biology. Essentially when we perceive the world as being different from the way we want it to be, we experience an urge to act—to do something to put the world right.

People's brains quickly notice and act on what is wrong in the world. People's brains do not notice what is right. There is no need to act. This urge helps us survive. It started back in the days when human beings lived in caves. People needed to immediately identify that the predatory cat they encountered, for example, was an enemy who wanted to hunt and eat them. Perceiving this, early human beings would quickly run away to seek shelter and safety. If their brains had not been set up to notice what was wrong, they might have seen the tiger and wondered if this pretty cat would make a good companion. That would have been the end of our ancestors and the end of us as a species. A modern-day example for today is that we notice the drivers on the road who drive dangerously and don't notice all of the safe, cooperative drivers who are also on the road with us.

We experience no urge to behave or do anything when the world is as we want it to be. When our stomachs are full; our lives are satisfying; and our relationships with our friends, family, and coworkers are running smoothly, we have no need to do anything. Life is good. In fact, when life is good, we don't even notice. We don't notice until something is wrong.

For instance, how does your head feel right now? How about your left knee? If you are not experiencing a headache or knee pain, you probably didn't give any thought to your head or your knee until your attention was directed to these body parts. On the other hand, when you have a stomachache, a sprained ankle, or worries about a broken relationship, you are constantly noticing and paying attention to them.

There is nothing wrong with you if you don't pay attention to the good parts of your life. That is the way your brain is set up. We pay attention and get signals driving us to action only when something is wrong.

● Notice what's right

Take a moment and think about the implications of this new information for you as a parent. What have you done well today? Have you hugged your child? Have you smiled and said "Good morning?" Did you take a minute to really appreciate your child, really look at her

parenting tip

 When Katie was a very little girl, her mother would write her special notes and put them in Katie's underwear drawer. In the beginning, she would write short notes telling Katie she loved her. To her mom's delight, Katie began to write notes too and place them in her mom's underwear drawer. As a young child, Katie's notes were drawings that she signed herself. As Katie grew and her writing skills improved, so did her notes. They didn't write a note every day, but for important or sensitive messages or at special times they would send each other a note.

One day Katie wrote a note telling her mom that the one hope she wished for in the entire world was for her mom to quit smoking. The mom had tried to quit before, but this time, bolstered with Katie's note, she decided to quit. So far, she has been successful.

This special ritual became an important avenue of communication for mother and daughter. You may want to try it with your children too.

with wonder and awe? If you did, good for you! You are noticing the positive aspects of your child and some of the beneficial results of your parenting practices. While you no doubt could easily recount your last big parenting mistake and the regret you have about it, you don't automatically notice your positive, effective parenting practices. As we have seen, this is because your brain is set up to process information from the negative feedback loops.

This pattern also applies to the behaviors of your child's that you notice and those that you don't notice. Take a moment to list all of the behaviors that your child has recently displayed that you wish would change. Perhaps your teenager's attitude has been sullen. Maybe your daughter argues every time you ask her to complete her chores. You notice without prompting all your child's actions that you wish were different and better.

Now list all those qualities that your child has that make you happy, that fill you with pride, that are amazing and show maturity beyond his years. These are not so easily listed. Why is that? The answer is not that there are fewer positive items to list. The answer is *your* brain. Your brain is set up to pay attention immediately to what is wrong. Your brain sees no need to pay attention to what is right. You have to consciously go out of your way, working against your brain, to find all the wonderful, appropriate, and effective aspects of your child's behavior.

Here's an example from a mother and daughter that will help you understand your brain and your relationships in a new way. When Sandra was twelve years old, she was constantly complaining and whining and seemed to be angry all the time. Shelly, her mother, was concerned because these new behaviors were occurring just as she was going through a divorce, remarrying, and creating a blended family.

She took her daughter to a wonderful counselor who said, "Oh, you are receiving the roses. Your daughter feels safe and secure enough with you to be herself, to be honest and forthright with you. She knows you will accept her and love her despite her complaining and whining. These are the roses of herself that she is sharing."

Shelly and her daughter now use this insight as a joke between them. Whenever Sandra is about to complain or argue, she warns her mother ahead of time, saying, "I'm about to share some roses with you, Mom."

● The conflict starts before your child is born

In addition to a lack of better models, the second reason parents hold on to the old model for parenting is fear. Here's why. As soon as we discover that we are going to be parents, we are already in conflict with our children. We want our children to mature into responsible adults, but more important is that we want our children to *survive* and live to become adults. Every decision we make as parents is based on our desire to keep our children safe and ensure their security and survival.

Even when we want our children to complete their homework assignments, we are worried about and considering their survival. "If my child doesn't do his homework, he may not succeed in school," says a parent. But if you question the parent further, you will discover a deeper level of fear. "If he doesn't succeed in school, he will have difficulty getting a good job and supporting himself. I want my child to be able to be competitive in the work world when he is grown up." For this parent, the child successfully completing his homework is one step in the direction of success and survival.

Because we are older, we have lived in the world longer and accumulated fears; whether justified or not, we worry about our children. Are they healthy? Are they learning? Do they have friends? Do they have the right friends? Are they working up to their appropriate grade level? Our worries seem endless.

On the other hand, safety and survival are the last concerns our children have when they enter the world. They are itching with curiosity.

Children are driven to explore, to discover, to eat, to touch, and to roll around in everything because of their curiosity.

Aren't you amazed by how often you tell your crawling baby, "No, don't touch that" or "Please don't put that in your mouth?" You know how quickly your young child can get into a perilous situation if you aren't watching every moment. Children are not old enough, don't know enough, and have not accumulated any fears about their world. They are simply curious, wanting to discover everything it has to offer.

As parents, then, we find ourselves in conflict with our children from the very beginning. We are trying to hold our children close to keep them safe. Our children are trying to break free of our hold to go out and discover the world. Our job is not to squelch our children's curiosity because we are frightened for their safety. We need to honor our children's desire to explore the world and to do so in ways that keep them safe. Because we are the adults, it is our job to teach our children how to be safe and survive without us.

If you attempt to restrict your children's activities too much because of your fear, chances are they will defy you and explore the world without your knowledge or consent. Children, driven by their inherent need for freedom, will not be held back!

Because you are frightened for your children, you may attempt to externally control and coerce them. But that external coercion only succeeds in creating tension between you and your child. It does not guarantee that your child will comply and remain safe. You may then be faced with a double fear:

- First, you may have a child who defies you and insists on exploring the world without your permission.
- Second, a child who does not know enough about keeping herself safe and who sneaks out without your permission and knowledge will probably face danger without you.

● Finding the yes in your no

Here is a useful idea to help you immediately practice your new knowledge about what moves your child toward growth and learning. And this will show you that despite the inherent conflict between fear and freedom that you and your child continually encounter, you can work out ways to honor both of your needs.

Have you ever noticed how frequently you say no to your child's requests? You are probably following a schedule. You have things to accomplish. If you take the time to honor your child's request and change plans, will you ever get all of your errands and chores completed? Yet no matter how often we deny children their requests, they still persist in asking for permission. Hope springs eternal.

See if you can change your automatic response of no when your child makes a request. Instead, see if you can find some points of yes within the no.

Here's the idea. Suppose your daughter asks if she can go swing on the swings at the playground today and you're sure that this outing will not fit into the day's schedule. Instead of just saying no, try telling her when you *can* take her next. Perhaps it won't be today, but maybe some free time is available for the swings on Saturday. So rather than simply answering no, you can tell her, "Yes, we will go to the park on Saturday morning."

Or, perhaps your son wants to buy a special rail car for his train set. You do not want to simply hand him the money, especially around this time of year when money seems to run shorter than the month. Instead of answering his request with a no, try saying, "Yes, we can figure out how to get that special car. You and I need to sit down, figure out a budget and a work schedule, and start a savings plan so that you can earn the money to purchase that car."

Of course, your answers in situations like these are not unconditional yesses, and your children will realize that too. However, your child will hear your answer of "Yes, and" differently from an unequivocal no even though "Yes, and here's how and when" is not the same as an unconditional yes. But it's much better than no with no option for change or hope.

Our job as parents is to help our children learn the responsible behaviors they need as we slowly increase the amount of freedom we grant them. When you find the yes in your no answers, you are seeking ways to help your child to learn and earn more responsible behaviors and more freedom.

When your son asks if he can have one more dessert after dinner, can you find a way to say yes? If your daughter wants to stay up later than her bedtime, can you find a part of your no answer that contains a yes?

● Conclusion

The usual methods of dealing with children and their behaviors need to change. These "common sense" and ineffective practices don't work to keep your children safe and may damage your relationship with them. While attempting to control your children, you will still be worried and frightened. In fact, now you know why your fears should increase.

Instead, work to create an environment where your child feels safe and can grow and learn. Work against your brain's negative feedback loop by noticing what is right in your world, with your child's behavior, and in your relationships. Instead of immediately and automatically saying no to your child's request, work to find ways to say "Yes, and" so that your child knows you are working with him to help him get more of what he wants.

This peaceful process of parenting relies on new science and new understandings of what motivates behavior. As you put these ideas into practice, they will become a more common process that you and your child will use more frequently and successfully.

parenting

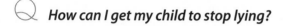

Q&A

Q *How can I get my child to stop lying?*

A The bad news is that you cannot make your child stop lying and begin telling the truth no matter how much you try or wish you could.

Now for some good news. You *can* influence your child's behavior. Here are some strategies you can try in an attempt to influence and guide your child to tell the truth and stop lying:

• Take your child's age into consideration. It is perfectly normal for preschoolers or younger children to make up stories as they explain their world. Remember that they believe in magic. Please refrain from accusing these young children of lying. That is a moral judgment that comes from your adult perspective. Young children do not yet have the cognitive developmental skills to know what lying means.

• Tell your children how important telling the truth is to you. Explain that when you tell each other the truth, you then know you can rely on and trust one another. Point out examples from your shared life experiences of when telling the truth had positive outcomes.

- Remember, all behavior is purposeful. Lying is no different. Children lie to get something they want. If children can learn ways to get what they want and need without lying, they will. As parents, your job is to ignore the behavior (though not easy) and realize that from the child's perspective the behavior is not the problem. Ask your child what she wants that she is trying to get by lying. Ask if she is willing to work with you to learn a better, more effective, and responsible way to get what she wants. If she agrees, then teach your child how to get what she wants without lying.

- At another time, continue the conversation about lying and telling the truth. As your child gets older and more mature, be sure that these discussions are two-way. Ask your child what he believes about lying. Does he know any people who lie? Share some times when telling the truth may have been particularly difficult for you.

Telling the truth is not behavior we are born with. Many adults continue to struggle to tell the truth, as our newspaper headlines indicate. By following the above strategies, parents improve the chances that their children will tell them the truth and that a loving, connected relationship between parents and their children will flourish.

2.

Your child was born with an instruction manual

You and your two-year-old are leaving the house for the day. You will drop her off at the child-care center on your way to work. As you walk out the door together, your mind is occupied with trying to keep track of all of the day's work and home activities. Because you and your daughter have been through this routine many times before, she knows the drill. Her job is to take your hand and walk straight to the car, jump into the backseat and into her car seat so you can help buckle her in safely.

But this morning something unusual happens. Instead of taking your hand, your daughter runs away from you, heading for the next-door neighbor's front yard. She is saying something as she runs, but you don't pay attention because you are frantically calling to her and chasing after her. *What is she doing? She is going to make me late! She knows better than to pull a stunt like this. Is this part of the terrible twos?*

Because her legs are shorter than yours, you are able to catch up to her quickly, even though you are clutching her backpack and your briefcase. You speak firmly to her, reprimanding her for not listening to you when you called her to come back. You carry her to the car, put her in her car seat, and buckle her in. During all of this, she is loudly crying, protesting, and arching her rigid body, making getting her into her seat even more difficult.

As you drive her to the child-care center, her temper tantrum and crying finally subside. What an upsetting way to start the day for you both!

● Your child's instruction manual

Even if your child is past the terrible twos, you probably recognize the story. You may be faced with a nine-year-old who doesn't seem to listen when you call him to dinner. Or perhaps your challenge occurs when you discover your thirteen-year-old stayed on the computer longer than your agreed-upon time limit.

This mother handled the situation pretty well. She didn't yell or scream. She didn't spank or threaten to punish. She simply got her daughter, picked her up, and proceeded with the day as planned. What's the harm?

It's worth taking a closer look at this typical parenting story. This mom thought: *What is she doing? She is going to make me late! She knows better than to pull a stunt like this. Is this part of the terrible twos?* She was only considering the situation from her own perspective. But when her daughter ran to the neighbor's yard, it had nothing to do with the mom or her vision of the day. This little girl did what she did because of her own needs. Although from the mother's perspective it looked like her daughter was running away from her, the child was running toward something that she was interested in. The child's behavior had nothing to do with her mother and everything to do with herself, her interests, and the drives she was born to follow.

Would you understand this better if you knew that there was a new kitten in the neighbor's yard? This little girl wanted to go investigate. All children are born with urges to behave, and this little girl was following her internal drive of curiosity. She experienced this impulse as an urge to learn, connect, and play with a potential new friend. Her thoughts were not preoccupied with the day's plans and tasks. She wasn't trying to make her mother late for work. She wasn't even thinking about her mother.

Are all children so thoughtless of their parents? Essentially, the answer is yes. But you might also make a case that the mother was being thoughtless of her child. Does that idea surprise you?

All human beings are born with vital impulses and needs, or internal instructions, that drive our behaviors. From birth until death, the reason behind all actions that every person takes is to follow one or more of these internal instructions. Human beings are internally motivated, driven by their biological and psychological needs. Everything that we do is an attempt to follow these instructions to try to satisfy our needs.

The biological instructions include the need for survival—the urge for air, water, food, shelter, sex, and elimination. All of these biological urges come from the genetic instructions we are born with to ensure that we will behave in ways that keep us alive. In order to actually experience this idea, why not test out your biological need for air? Dive underwater at a swimming pool. If you stay underwater long enough, eventually you will experience an overwhelming urge to get your head above the water so you can breathe air. Your biological instruction for survival is at work. You have an urge to behave so that you can breathe air continuously.

Included in the biological instruction for survival is also the psychological need to feel safe and secure. Most of us feel safe and secure most of the time. But you may have a heightened awareness of these psychological aspects of the survival urge when you are traveling to an unknown area, sleeping overnight in an unfamiliar hotel, or experiencing a near mishap while driving your car. These feelings of wanting to take action, such as locking your car doors or your hotel door, are based on your urge to behave in ways that will keep you safe and secure and help you survive.

The other genetic instructions that you will become very familiar with are psychological in nature. These include

- The need for love and belonging
- The need for power
- The need for fun
- The need for freedom

Much of the conflict we experience with our children arises from the way they pursue the fulfillment of their needs.

● All behavior is purposeful

If you spend any time with children you will see many examples of when they are following their genetic instructions irresponsibly. For instance, ask a class of third graders to form a line. Inevitably, one child will push and shove others so that he can be in the front of the line. This is an example of a child following his drive for power and fun. His behavior is purposeful, and this child might even be successful in getting to the front of the line using this aggressive and physical method.

However, pushing and shoving are examples of a child's irresponsible behaviors. Behaving responsibly means that a person is behaving to follow a genetic instruction to meet one or more needs in ways that do not interfere with other people's ability to follow their genetic instructions and meet their needs.

In the example of the third grader who wants to stand at the front of the line, his behavior is purposeful and effective but irresponsible, so it is the job of an adult to help him learn how to effectively get what he wants while acting responsibly. The best way to do this is by teaching, not punishing, threatening, or scolding. Remember, he is born with the urge to behave. But he is not born with the innate knowledge about how to follow these urges responsibly. This child does not decide to be a bully, pushing and shoving his way to get what he wants. He simply does not know any more effective and responsible ways to achieve his goal and follow his instruction other than what he is doing.

Once you understand that your child is born with genetic instructions that she experiences as urges to behave, you will view your child's behavior differently. Even though it may appear as if your child is acting out against your wishes or to spite you, this is not true. Your child's behavior is prompted by her desire for love, power, fun, or freedom. Your child is behaving for herself, in accordance with her genetic instructions.

As parents we understand and accept this idea quite readily when our children are infants. We don't scold or blame our babies for crying when they are hungry or cold. Crying is one of the few behaviors babies

parenting tip

f a baby has been fed, burped, and is wearing a dry diaper but continues to cry, don't ask why he is crying. Instead, try softly whispering in his ear. Because the baby can't hear you, he will stop crying to listen.

are born with. It is the only way they can follow their urges to get more of what they want and need. It would be odd to hear parents label their infant as a strong-willed, uncooperative child. Babies must learn other ways to follow their genetic urges to get what they want. Parents patiently teach their infants to communicate with them as the infants grow into babies and beyond. Unfortunately, we somehow seem to forget or lose sight of this idea as an infant matures.

Another factor to consider is that our lives are complicated because we are dealing with more than one human being—at the very least our own drives in addition to our child's. Even if parents' only job in life was to attend to their children, complications would still arise. But parents are involved in their own lives as well. Parents also are driven by genetic instructions. Remember when your infant wouldn't sleep, and you were desperate for sleep? You loved your baby. You tried hard to be patient, kind, loving, and understanding, but you experienced a huge urge to sleep anyway—even though your baby may not have.

All behavior is purposeful. The purpose for all behavior is that we are attempting to follow our genetic instructions, our genetic drives, and meet our needs. What is your purpose for reading this book? Perhaps you are following an urge to feel more competent as a parent, helping you to meet your need for power. My purpose for writing this book is to share ideas and information with you, attempting to influence your parenting methods. I am following my urge for power.

The reason the toddler ran away from her mother and toward the kitten was that the child was following her urges for fun and love and belonging by trying to meet and play with a new friend. The reason the mother was chasing, scolding, and maneuvering her daughter to the car was that she was following her drive for power by accomplishing her morning commute competently and her drive for freedom by choosing where she was going and how she was going to get there.

● Stop asking why

Why does my child act that way? Why doesn't my child listen to me? Why does he keep asking me permission when I've already told him no?

Here's good news for all parents everywhere: you no longer need to ask any of these kinds of questions. You never need to wonder why your child is doing something or not doing something else! Here is the answer. And if you can believe it, this is *always* the answer.

Children (and all people) do what they do because they are born with genetic drives for safety, love, power, fun, and freedom. Conversely, children (and all people) don't do what they don't do because they are born with genetic urges for safety, love, power, fun, and freedom. Children (and all people) experience these instructions as an urge to behave in ways that will satisfy those needs.

You never have to wonder again. If you want to know why your child is behaving a certain way, know that she is trying to attain safety, power, love, fun, and freedom. You never have to ask your child *why* again.

The reason for *all* behavior is people's best attempts to follow their instructions for safety, love, power, fun, and freedom. This is always the answer to why.

● The magical question

Here is a better and more helpful question to ask. You can ask either yourself or your child: *What is it my child wants that she is behaving in such an inappropriate way to try to get?* You now know the motivation for all behavior (the basic needs), but what you don't know is what your child wants and needs. He is trying to get this mysterious want by behaving the way he is behaving.

This question is magical because once you know to ask it, you can find out what your child wants. Then you can teach your child a more effective, appropriate, and responsible way to get what she wants. By changing the question you ask your child (or yourself), you will change direction and find better solutions.

The next time you hear yourself asking, "Why is my child acting that way?" change the question. Ask instead, "I wonder what my child wants that he is trying to get by acting that way? My job is to help him learn a more effective, responsible way to get what he wants."

Just for fun, practice asking this magical question everywhere:

- The next time you hear a political speech, ask yourself, *I wonder what that politician wants that she is trying to get by making this speech?*
- The next time you observe another person's crazy driving, ask yourself, *I wonder what that person wants that he is trying to get by speeding?*
- The next time you hear another parent ask his child why, ask yourself, *I wonder what that father wants that he is trying to get by asking his child why?*

When using this question with your child be sure to ask just this way: "What do you want that you are trying to get by acting that way?" Even though this is an awkward, grammatically incorrect question, your child will answer this magical question and together you can help her learn more effective and responsible behaviors to get what she wants.

Once you stop asking why and start asking "What do you want?" your parenting practices will become much easier and more effective!

● From terrible to terrific

Have you noticed that for a period of time your child is a perfect angel, and then seemingly overnight she can become "hell on wheels"? Beginning at around eighteen months, children alternate between a cooperative stage and a competitive stage. This roller-coaster ride never ends, even in adulthood, but the periods within each stage become longer and less dramatic. When your child leaves your home to make his way in the world as a young adult, you have less need to develop coping strategies for these changing patterns.

When your child is in the competitive stage, her needs for power and freedom are the strongest instructions driving her behavior. The stage of the terrible twos is one most parents are familiar with. The reason parents call it terrible is that children are trying to gain power over and freedom from their parents.

Happily, the competitive stage is followed by a cooperative stage, when love and fun are the strongest needs driving his behavior. Because your child wants to feel loved and connected with you and have fun with you, he is very cooperative. You can fail to notice this important and terrific phase because you expect your children will cooperate with you all the time. Remember also, because your brain notices what is wrong, not what is right, you should make a conscious effort to pay attention and celebrate when your child is in the wonderful, cooperative phase of his development, as those times are some of the most fun and rewarding.

Interestingly, even when a child is in the competitive stage, if she is not feeling safe, she will rely on cooperative behaviors. This can help you understand why your argumentative child cooperates with the babysitter, eats so well when spending the weekend with her grandmother, or is the best helper in her second-grade class. Although it may not feel like it, the fact that your child trusts you enough to practice and learn competitive behaviors to effectively meet her needs for power and freedom is good news. That's why she argues with you and, seemingly, no one else.

When children reach their preteen and adolescent years and their safety is threatened, they rely on competitive behaviors. That's why a teenager will argue with an adult in the face of overwhelming evidence that he is wrong. In order to feel safe he needs to be right, to win, and to competitively meet his needs for power and freedom no matter what.

Here are some ways you can help ease the pain during the awful times when your children are driven to compete and are driving you crazy:

- Acknowledge, accept, and be happy about it. Remember that these behaviors will serve your children well in young adulthood when they will need to make their own decisions. For example, these learned competitive behaviors will help teenagers resolve to make a sage choice in a dangerous situation, like not getting into a car with someone who has been drinking.

- Give your child more choices and more opportunities to be in charge. For example, a family was having problems when they took their four-year-old grocery shopping. She always wanted something the parents didn't want to buy. The parents put the daughter in charge of gathering items from Mom's list to put in her own cart. It worked like a charm. She completely forgot about the items she originally wanted.

- Pay attention to the cooperative times and celebrate them with your child. Acknowledge with a smile that your child is with you today. Plan a special picnic on the living room floor when it is raining outside, or simply tell others how wonderful your child is acting while your child is within range to hear the compliment.

Know that your children will go back and forth between the competitive and cooperative stages about every six months between ages two and seven. From seven to twelve, the flip-flop between both stages extends to approximately eight months. During adolescence each stage lasts about nine months. Embrace the happy, terrific moments as well as the combative, terrible ones because they are natural parts of your child's process of learning to function successfully in the world.

● Becoming a conscious parent

What time have you set as your children's bedtime? How did you arrive at this time? Is there a homework rule at your house, such as a time when you expect your children to complete their homework? Why did you decide to make this the rule? Do you have dessert rules at your house? Are these rules the same for the grown-ups in the house as they are for the children? Why did you decide to make these rules?

Most of us do day-to-day routines the way they have always been done, whether those routines involve parenting, driving to work, baking a cake, decorating the Christmas tree, or planning the menu for our Thanksgiving meal. Many of your parenting guidelines probably are derived from how your parents ruled, guided, and parented you. The strongest role models we have for parenting are our own parents.

peaceful parenting quiz

- ● What household rules have you established for your children?
- ● Where did they come from?
- ● Do you agree with each one?
- ● Is it time to change some of the rules in your home?

Observe your own parenting responses carefully because this role modeling may not even be in your awareness.

I clearly remember a time when my son Paul accused me of loving his brother, David, more than I loved him. Without any thought or hesitation I answered, "You're absolutely right." Where did that response come from? With a little reflection I could hear my own mother saying the same thing to me when I accused her of loving one of my sisters more than she loved me. After giving it more thought, I decided that this was as satisfactory an answer as any. What I found equally amazing was how quickly and automatically I gave my answer. There was no planning, forethought, or preparation for such an event with my child, yet there was my mother, immediately involved with my parenting response and decision.

Parenting is an incredibly rewarding job, but it's not easy. So much of what we do as parents is based on ideas and notions that we may not even be aware of. Much of what we do as parents is related to how our parents did their job with us. Our parents may not have used bad parenting practices, but another question is, are they relevant practices? When our parents were raising their children (us), the world was very different from how it is today.

Whether you have resolved to parent as well as your parents did or you have decided that you never want to be the kind of parent to your children that your parents were to you, you can't change your parenting practices until you first become conscious of what you are doing as a parent. So many choices and decisions that you make are not based on a thoughtful decision but rather on an unmindful response.

Your three-year-old asks if she can have a piece of chewing gum. Your answer, seeming to come from nowhere, is "Not until you're five years old." Where did that rule come from? Is there some book of universal child-rearing rules that lays down that law? Upon further reflection, you may realize that this was the rule your father gave you and you are

parenting tip

What can a woman do when she's out with young boys who need to use a public restroom? When they are younger, taking them into the ladies' room is fine, but when they get older, it's inappropriate, yet she can't take them into the men's room.

One aunt uses a solution she says she found in Dear Abby. She now sends her nephews into the men's room together, asking them to sing at the top of their lungs while she waits for them just outside of the men's room. She knows that as long as she can hear them singing, everything is fine. This solution works for all of them.

passing it on to your children. Are you sure that you want to do that?

This may not be a bad answer or rule, but is it one that you believe in? Or are you simply giving the first answer that pops into your head when your child asks you a question that you are not prepared to answer?

Children are masters at asking questions the answers to which we haven't been thoughtful about or taken the time to reflect on. When that happens we fall back on the answers we were given as children.

"You must keep your commitment to the club you have joined for at least a year. If you decide that you want to quit next year, you can. But once you've made a commitment, you must see it through." This may have been the guidance your parents gave you, but is it a tradition you want to continue? There isn't a correct answer here. Take the time to question and decide whether or not you believe in a rule that you are automatically enforcing simply because you learned it from your parents.

The first step to becoming a more competent parent is to become a *conscious* parent. In order to choose a different path from the one you were given, you must first become aware of the path you have been on—the actions you have been taking. Next, you need a plan for how you will behave differently.

You may have no idea of how you could change this habit of unconscious parenting. Here is a process that you can follow to help you move toward being more conscious and more competent. Well removed from the upsetting situation, ask yourself these questions:

- What automatic behavior did I use to handle the frustration?
- Was I conscious of what I was doing at the time?
- Do I want to behave differently next time?
- If yes, what are the many different alternative choices available to me?
- Of these choices, which option will I choose next time?

Once you have responded differently, take time to reflect and evaluate your new response. Did it help you? Did it help the situation? Do you want to repeat this new response or plan another option?

Why not take time to reflect on the rules and regulations you are using when guiding your own children? In case you are not aware of the rules, regulations, and guidelines you have set down for your children, ask them. Children will be quick to list each and every rule, especially if they realize you are considering changing some. You may discover that you are satisfied with most of the choices and decisions you are making. You may also discover that some of the rules your parents made for you no longer apply to you and your children.

● Conclusion

Don't wait. Sometime before today is over, one of your children will misbehave. Seize this opportunity to practice your new skill of teaching your children to behave responsibly while following their needs. Ask the magical question, "What do you want that you are trying to get by misbehaving?" Remember, your job is to teach your children how to follow their genetic instructions for safety, love, power, fun, and freedom responsibly. Each time your child misbehaves she is attempting to fulfill one or more of her needs. She just doesn't know how to do it any other way than by misbehaving. Take advantage of this perfect opportunity to teach your child something when she most wants to learn it. Whether your child is in the terrific, cooperative stage or the terrible, competitive stage, follow your urge to teach your child by using the magical question and working each situation out together.

Sometime today when your children are behaving cooperatively, responsibly, and well, spend the quiet time becoming more conscious. What rules do you have in your home? Are these helpful and useful? Can you eliminate those rules that you are carrying on from tradition but that don't help anyone in your home?

parenting
Q&A

Q *My twelve-year-old daughter, Sheila, seems to spend too much time moping around the house. When I talked with her about it, she told me she was unhappy. I asked her, "What is it you want that you are trying to get by spending unhappy time at home?" She told me that she wants a best friend. How can I help her?*

A As overwhelmed and inadequate as you may feel, there is good news. She is willing to discuss her upsetting and important life issue with you. You have been given a huge compliment and advantage. Please take the time to notice and be grateful that your daughter trusts you and still talks with you as she enters her adolescent years.

Your first step is to get curious. Discover more about her current friends. Who are they and what qualities do they have that she is attracted to? Is there someone in particular that she is interested in having as her best friend? Ask her about the particular people who are important to her. Listen carefully to her answers.

Next, ask her to play detective. Does she know what makes

people friends with each other? Does she know what makes a best friend different from other friends? Encourage her to research and investigate the whole concept and situation.

Simultaneously, work with Sheila to discover what she likes about herself. Does she think she would make a good friend for someone else to have? Is she interesting? Is she kind? What types of interests does she have? Does she have any interests she would be willing to share with a best friend? Essentially, what you are doing is helping Sheila to develop a loving friendship with herself. This isn't the same as a best friend, but it is very important and something she can control.

Once she has some specific answers to the friendship and best-friendship question, work with her to develop a plan. What does Sheila think that she could do to begin culti-vating more friends? Together, brainstorm many ideas. Once you have a list of ideas, decide which one she would like to start with. Ask her how you can be helpful.

Help her by listening sympathetically and then assist her in solving this problem as you would any other problem. Although you may want to dive into expressing great empathy and doting-love to comfort her, that will be helpful for only a limited period of time. Instead, treat this as a problem that can be solved, lend enthusiasm to the challenge by posing ques-tions like, "Isn't it a funny thing that some people are friends with each other but not other people? I wonder why this is?" Do you see how different that is from, "Oh, you poor darling! Girls your age just don't know what they're missing out ▶

parenting

Q&A

on by not being your best friend"? The first statement creates an interesting, solvable challenge. The latter creates a pitiable circumstance in which Sheila is a victim. Aim for the first.

One final hint: Avoid telling Sheila your own war stories. Although you may believe you're showing sympathy and understanding, your daughter just doesn't believe it. Adolescents are much more interested in their own sorry circumstances, conundrums, and challenges. After you spend time working with Sheila, understanding what she wants, creating a plan for success, and then acting on the plan to move her toward success, then you can ask her if she would like to hear your similar stories about friends and best friends. Then she might be interested. But if she isn't, relax and know that eventually she will be more interested in the ancient history that she sees as your life.

3.

Every parent has ESP

Every day after school my sons, Paul and David, would come bounding into the house, drop their backpacks in the middle of the kitchen floor, and move on to bigger and better things, like changing their clothes for a basketball game or a home-run derby tournament. Every day I would greet them and before long remind them to "please put your backpacks away." This pattern never varied. I had one goal in mind—keeping the kitchen in relative order. Paul and David had another idea in their minds—freedom from school meant time for play. Thinking back on this, I wonder why I never tried a strategy other than requests for compliance that sometimes turned into nagging. After all, I knew the conflict was coming because it happened every day.

● You can predict the future

At this very moment, can't you predict the next time you will get into some kind of a disagreement or conflict with your child? All parents already know the situations they will face where children will want one thing and parents will want another. Wouldn't it be wonderful if you could handle those predictable situations differently?

You already know when your child is most likely to misbehave. You know the time of day, the place, and the circumstances. How did you get to be so smart? Because you have experienced the situation before. Don't wait for it to happen again. Make a plan now.

Sometime this week when there is a tension-free moment between you and your child, talk about the situation. Share with your child how you want the scenario to play out. Ask your child how he wants the interaction to go. If necessary, review with each other what your agreed-upon rules are for this particular situation. Then make a plan for a successful outcome that gives everyone more of what they each want.

● The homework hassle

To help make this process clearer, here's an example. Perhaps you are a parent who can predict that asking your child to do her homework guarantees the beginning of another huge conflict. How do you know this? Because for the past weeks, months, and years—since your fifth grader was in the third grade—this is what has happened every time you mentioned homework to her. Here is what you will do differently.

Saturday at lunch, while you and your daughter are enjoying eating peanut butter and jelly sandwiches together, here is the type of conversation you will have:

MOTHER: You know, Felicity, I would like to work out a different plan with you for how you begin to do your homework on our weekday evenings. I would love it if I could mention or remind you about your homework, and you didn't yell or get angry. I can imagine that you would smile at me and tell me you were just about to go and do your homework on your own. If you and I could work out a plan for beginning your homework in a way that would please you, how would it go?

FELICITY: You know, Mom, I can remember to do my homework on my own without you having to remind me. If things went the way I wanted, you would never mention my homework ever again. You would trust me and assume that I had done what I needed to do instead of bugging me, nagging me, and not trusting me.

MOTHER: I had no idea that you felt that way. I don't want to be a nag or give you the impression that I don't trust you. But I feel that part of my job as your mother is to be sure you are doing your schoolwork. How can we work this out so I know you have done your work and you know I trust you?

FELICITY: How about if I tell you when I'm done?

MOTHER: Okay. But sometimes we have plans for the evening, and I don't want them to interfere with your homework time.

FELICITY: How about if you tell me when we have plans so I can work my own homework time around them? I can still tell you when I'm done.

MOTHER: That sounds good. How do you want me to handle it if you forget to tell me or you don't tell me? How can I ask in a way that doesn't sound like nagging?

FELICITY: You could ask me, "Felicity, is there something you want to tell me?"

MOTHER: Okay. And if you look at me blankly, I'll say, "You remember, something about your *h.w.*"

FELICITY: Okay. Good.

This sounds wonderful, doesn't it? But be prepared. Your great plan will probably *not work* the first time. Know this in advance. However, don't give up. Perseverance is the key to your success.

Your child will probably revert to the old, unsuccessful habits. You will be tempted to revert to your familiar patterns of nagging, perhaps now adding the dig that you and your child had an agreement that she is not living up to. Despite your strong temptations, do not give in to them.

Simply wait until another time when you and your child are feeling loving or neutral toward one another and bring the topic up again. Repeat that you are still interested in coming up with a plan together so that you both are able to get what you want. Ask your child if your original plan was a good one. Do either of you think you need to modify the plan in some way? Add the contingency plan of how you will act and what you will say if your child doesn't do what she is agreeing to now. Then do your best to follow the plan again.

Be prepared. The plan still might not work the second time. Your strongest strategy, however, is to continue to talk to your child about how the two of you are going to work this out. If you can remain interested in solving the problem together without accusations or recriminations of any sort, eventually you and your child will be able to successfully solve this problem.

parenting tip

The "I'm bored" jar

When your children complain, "I'm bored. What can I do?" you need an "I'm bored" jar. Here's how to make one.

Clean out an old coffee tin or mayonnaise jar. Help the children decorate it with magazine pictures and family photos that show everyone having fun.

Ask your children to make a list of activities that they enjoy doing, particularly activities they can do alone. Cut apart the list so that each idea is on a separate strip of paper. Fill the jar with these ideas.

Additionally, when you observe your children engaged in some activity that they really enjoy, write it down and add it to the jar. Ask them to do the same. In fact, you can review and solicit ideas during a family meal and add more to the jar every couple of days.

Here are some ideas to help you get started:

Listen to favorite music	Go for a bike ride
Paint a picture	Plan a trip
Work a puzzle	Practice card tricks
Bake cookies	

The next time the children complain that there's nothing to do, have them pick an activity from the jar.

● Quality world pictures

If you are like most parents, instead of using your ability to predict and prepare for the next argument with your child, you probably hope for the best. You hope your child will have changed so that the two of you won't need to get into the same argument again.

But you've probably already discovered that relying on hope isn't enough. The reason can be explained by a concept called *quality world pictures.* While people often share the same genetic drives for safety, love, power, fun, and freedom, each person develops unique and specific pictures of how these needs will be met. In the example, Mom wants to meet her need for power by seeing herself as a competent mother who helps her daughter successfully complete her homework. Felicity wants to meet her needs for power and freedom by completing her homework independently without her mother interfering or monitoring her actions. Each of them has a specific and unique quality world picture of how she will meet her needs for power and freedom. Mom and Felicity did not have conflicting needs, they had conflicting quality world pictures.

When you and your child have different quality world pictures, the first step toward resolving your difficulties is to spend time reflecting on your quality world picture—what you want. Share this with your children. The next step is to ask your children what their quality world pictures are—what they want. Then together you can work to find a solution that allows you all to get some of your quality world pictures fulfilled. This process will help you all successfully and harmoniously meet your needs.

● Don't give up

Judy, mother of seven-year-old John and five-year-old Molly, had a terrible time every school day morning. She would attempt to awaken the children in time for them to eat breakfast, get dressed, and be ready in time for her to drive them to school. Every morning was the same. She called the children to wake up and get moving. They remained in bed. She called to them repeatedly, until finally she would go into each child's bedroom and scream at them and make threats about what would happen if they didn't get up and get going. This was not how Judy wanted school mornings to start for her children or herself. After hearing me describe the quality world picture strategy, she thought she would give it a try.

Much to Judy's surprise, she discovered that John and Molly had such a difficult time getting out of bed on school mornings because they didn't want to get up and go directly to school. They wanted time to play in the morning first, before they went to school. This information really surprised Judy. She thought the children wanted to sleep longer. But upon reflection she realized that the children had no trouble getting up early on Saturdays and Sundays. Of course on Saturdays and Sundays, they got out of bed and played.

Using this new information, she and the children made a plan. In order for them to get up and play and still have enough time for breakfast and to get ready for school, they would have to get out of bed forty-five minutes earlier. Both children assured her that this was a fine plan for them, as long as they got to play first.

The first morning of their new plan seemed just like the old arrangement, except that now Judy was asking, nagging, and pleading with the children to get up for an additional forty-five minutes. It was hard not to make threats, but she resisted, telling them, "If you don't get up now, you won't be able to play before school."

As they drove to school together she asked the children how they each thought the new plan worked. Everybody, including Judy, agreed that the new plan was not successful that morning. But both John and Molly reassured their mother that getting up early to play was still something they were interested in and that there was no need to change the plan or make a new one.

On day two of the plan, the results were the same. Judy still felt tempted to threaten the children but resisted.

As they drove to school together, Judy once again asked the children to evaluate the success of the plan. Again, all agreed that it was not working. Again, the children reassured their mother that getting up to play before school was something they wanted. So they all agreed they would try again the next day.

This went on for two weeks! But finally they succeeded. When I asked Judy how she found the stamina to continue this process with her children for two weeks, she told me, "First, you told me to expect that the plan wouldn't work initially. So I knew I wasn't doing anything wrong, that failure was simply an expected part of the new process. Second, I felt as though I had nothing to lose. Mornings were so horrible that I thought continuing to ask the children to help me solve the problem could only get us to better mornings."

● Finding solutions

Remember, all behavior is purposeful, and all behavior is our best attempt to get what we need and want. Rarely do our children want to annoy, ignore, or infuriate us. That doesn't mean that our children's behavior isn't annoying and infuriating, but that is almost never the purpose behind their behavior. They are doing what they are doing because of what they each want and need. Although you can probably identify several of the errors that each parent makes in the quiz below, the point is that each of these children does not do anything that is directed against the parent.

When our children want something different from what we want

Here are some examples of typical disagreements that arise between parents and children. Using this peaceful parenting process, see if you can identify what the parent wants, what the child wants, and how each situation might be resolved. Take this opportunity to parent differently. During this exercise you won't have the same emotional attachment and involvement you have when dealing with your own children.

Example 1: At the end of a long, difficult day, you are in the kitchen working hard to prepare dinner and get it on the table. Not only are you feeling tired, but you are fully aware that everyone needs food soon, or one or more of your children will experience a "meltdown" from fatigue and low blood sugar. When dinner is almost ready, you ask your eight-year-old son to "please set the table." No response. You ask again. Still no response. Finally, you accuse him of laziness and selfishness, angrily telling him to come and set the table, and he complies.

Example 2: The weekend has finally arrived. As usual you have set aside Saturday morning for cleaning, straightening, ▶

and completing weekly household chores that have been put off during the week.

Confident that your eleven-year-old daughter is cleaning her room, compiling her laundry, and changing her sheets, you concentrate your efforts on tackling the mess in the kitchen. Finally, you go to her bedroom to check her progress. Much to your horror, you see your daughter still in bed, sleeping. *How lazy! She'll do anything to get out of helping you clean on a Saturday.* Furiously and loudly you insist she get out of bed and start cleaning.

Example 3: Running late, you hurry to the school to pick up your fourteen-year-old as the two of you had planned. Although you are only a few minutes late, your child is not in sight. *Where is she?* You park the car and go into the building. You can't find her. You go into the office and ask one of the secretaries if she has seen your daughter. When she tells you she hasn't, you really begin to worry. Were you so late that she took a ride with someone else? She wouldn't be foolish enough to get into a stranger's car, would she? Just as you are on the verge of panic, you see your daughter come around the corner of the building, smiling and laughing with her friends.

Your rage is as large as your worry had been only moments before. You let her have it, telling her that you and she had a plan. You expected her to be where she said she would be, when she said she would be there. You accuse her of being thoughtless and selfish. How could she have put you through such worry? You fail to mention to her that you were also late.

them to want, we are annoyed and irritated. But when you were eight years old, did you care about setting the dinner table so that the family could eat? Did you ever want to spend Saturdays, your free day, helping to clean the house? During your middle school years, was your first priority to be sure you didn't keep one of your parents waiting for you?

In these three examples each of these desires is what the parents want, not what the child wants. As the parents, we don't need to relinquish our wants and give in to satisfy our children's wants. We do need to understand and accept that we want our children to want the same results that we do (a timely dinner, a clean house, a child ready to be picked up). Sometimes we are lucky, and our children's wants coincide with ours. Many times our children are not even thinking about—let alone accepting, or rejecting—what we want. They are too busy concentrating on what they want.

So if you find yourself labeling your child as lazy, inconsiderate, selfish, or any other less-than-flattering names, stop. Whether you are saying these labels out loud or thinking them, these names will do nothing to enhance your relationship with your child. They also won't inspire your child to behave differently. (For further discussion on the subject see "Language, Labels, and Results" in appendix B.)

Instead, realize that at that moment what you want and what your child wants are probably two different things. Share with your child what you want and ask for assistance. If appropriate, ask your child what she wants and negotiate a solution that allows you both to get what you want.

Here are some suggestions for responses the parents in the quiz could have had to each situation.

Example 1

"I want us all to eat dinner soon. Would you please help by setting the table?"

Example 2

"Saturday is my day to clean. What do you want your Saturdays to be like? I need you to clean your room, but if Saturday isn't the day you want to do it, can we work out a different schedule? I don't really care when you do it, I just want it to be done."

Example 3

"I was late coming to pick you up. When I saw you weren't here, I got scared that something bad had happened to you. I'm glad you're safe; I'm sorry I was late. I'll be on time next time. Will you?"

parenting tip

Do you have a child who throws temper tantrums? This tip may help you and your child cope with them. Find a special area rug and make this the temper tantrum rug. Each time your child begins his tantrums, either carry him or direct him to the rug.

Instead of resisting the behaviors that you don't want to see in your children, create the framework and the boundaries where it is okay for them to behave as they want.

Once you stop trying to control or resist your children's behaviors, they will be more willing and ready to work things out with you.

● Conclusion

Use your ESP to predict that this process may take many failures before you and your child are able to complete a plan successfully. Hang in there and try not to resort to the old, ineffective habits that failed to get your children to behave as you wanted them to. Know that your children are doing what they are doing for their own very good reasons, based on their quality world pictures and genetic drives. Work with your children to develop plans for success and believe that success will come—eventually.

parenting
Q&A

Q *My six-year-old son, Sean, constantly interrupts. My husband and I have discussed with Sean the importance of listening and waiting, but he still seems to need to get all of my attention by interrupting. Any suggestions?*

A During a time when you, your husband, and son are all feeling happy and well connected with one another, bring up the topic of your son's interrupting. Repeat your previous explanation of manners and why it is important for your son to wait his turn. But here is the key. Tell your son that you want to create a special hand signal as a reminder not to interrupt. Tell him that this is going to be a secret code that only the three of you will know. Ask him to help come up with a signal and really make a game of this. Try out many different alternatives, being sure to include silly and outrageous ideas—the sillier the better. This will help your son get into the spirit of the game.

After spending time exploring and creating alternatives and no doubt laughing a lot as you do, the three of you need to decide on only one. Unless it is too outrageous, it might help if your son chooses the hand signal he likes best. Then the three of you need to practice making this signal. Pretend that you and your husband are involved in a conversation and have Sean pretend to interrupt. Then, either you or your husband or both give Sean the hand signal. Continue the practice and role playing with you and Sean talking and your husband interrupting, then with your husband and Sean talking and you interrupting. The next step is to use this hand signal in real-life situations.

Remember that using the hand signal will probably fail the first few times that you try it. If Sean interrupts and forgets what the hand signal means, tell him verbally that you would appreciate his waiting and not interrupting. Then later, when the two of you are alone, remind him of your agreement to use the hand signal. Practice the signal again, keeping the mood as light and playful as possible.

If you consistently use the hand signal during these times and discuss the plan in private when the hand signal doesn't work, repeating these steps as many times as it takes, eventually you, your husband, and Sean will have great success with this plan.

4.

Because I said so, that's why!

How do I get my child to start eating vegetables? How do I get my child to start doing his homework? How do I get my child to complete her chores? How do I get my child to stop hitting his brother? How do I get my child to stop using swear words? How do I get my child to stop whining?

So many of the questions that parents ask fall into one or both of these categories: *How do I get my child to start doing something?* Or *How do I get my child to stop doing something?*

Conventional wisdom recommends that you find out what your child's currency is and use it as your carrot (reward) or stick (withholding or withdrawing the child's desires as punishment). If you've tried this method, you probably said something like this: "If you behave well at your doctor's appointment today, then we can go to McDonald's for a treat." Or "If you don't stop teasing your little brother, then you won't be allowed to have any dessert after dinner tonight."

Generally speaking, the template for the typical parent statement sounds like this: "If you do what I want, then I'll give you something you desire," or "If you don't stop doing what I don't want you to do, then I will withhold or withdraw something you desire." These standard "if-then" statements are all attempts to control your children using threats or rewards.

How to Be a Great Parent offers very different solutions because it starts from a very different understanding of you and your child. We will look at the theory first, and then we'll get into the practical application.

● Why won't my children do what I ask them to?

As you now know, your child and you are born with psychological instructions for safety and security, love and belonging, power, fun, and freedom. Remember also that each of us develops very specific quality world pictures of what we want in our world, and we follow these drives to meet our needs. We behave in certain ways in an attempt to get whatever it is we want that will meet our needs and follow our genetic impulses. All behavior is purposeful. All of our actions are attempts to try to change the world so it will be the way we want it to be.

If each of us lived in the world alone, we might have greater success in getting more of what we want because our quality world pictures would not conflict with anyone else's. However, we would be lonely and unable to satisfactorily meet our need for love and belonging.

As parents, we have ideas that our children should do their homework, eat their vegetables, and complete their chores without being reminded to do those things. And of course in our quality world picture our children would never annoy a sibling, whine, or swear. These quality world pictures of our children behaving as we want them to satisfy our genetic instructions to be powerful, successful parents who nurture and love our responsible children.

Anytime your child starts behaving contrary to these pictures or ideals, you experience the urge to behave in a way that attempts to change your child to become what you want.

Remember that your child is born with these same drives although she is not born knowing how to follow these drives responsibly. Even though you have taught her to behave responsibly, she still may behave irresponsibly. Children discover that behaving irresponsibly may be more effective in getting them what they want, even if their behavior is against your rules.

When parents ask how they can get their child to start doing this particular behavior or stop doing another, essentially parents are asking how they can get their child to behave in a way that will satisfy their quality world picture of how they want their child to behave. They want to know how they can get their child to want the same quality world picture that they want.

Why won't your child just do what you have asked him to do? Wouldn't it be wonderful if every time you said to your child, "Go clean your room," your child immediately stopped doing whatever it was that he was doing and went to his room, stayed there for a reasonable period of time, and then asked you to come for inspection? Can you imagine that? Or how about this? You ask your child if he has any homework, and he tells you that he has already completed it and asks if you would like to go over it with him to be sure that he hasn't made any errors. What if you called all members of your family to dinner and they came and sat down with hands and faces washed, smiling and asking if they could help bring dinner to the table?

Perhaps this sounds like exactly the life you have been dreaming of. But now let's take this same notion of mild-mannered compliance and apply it to different situations. Imagine that your teenage son is out with some friends who ask him to steal liquor from the family liquor cabinet, and your son happily obliges. Or suppose that your daughter is asked to smoke a cigarette, and she happily goes along with this suggestion. Or what if your child's friend suggests that together they cheat on a school exam, and your child complies willingly? You would not feel as pleased about your child complying in these situations as you would about your child's willingness to obey your wishes.

parenting tip

When was the last time you offered the gift of uninterrupted and undivided attention to your child? Perhaps now is the time to implement this as a daily practice.

Our days are so busy and filled with organizing our children, our homes, our lives. Who has time to actually listen to your daughter as you are asking your son to find his shoes, making everyone's lunch, and finding the missing library books that are due today?

Try this: Greet your child as she comes home from school. When you sit with her to eat an afternoon snack, tell her you want to listen to all she has to share with you. Then listen with a smile. Or, each night as you put your child to bed, before you read the

Your child is developing a mind and determination of his own. This starts when your child is born, when he decides he is hungry, has slept long enough, or needs his father's loving cuddles and hugs. And this same self-determination continues throughout your child's life into independence and adulthood.

Our heart's desire is that our children develop into independent, responsible adults. So when did you think this process was going to begin? Did you imagine that your child would always comply with your commands and wishes, but then assert her independence with all of the other people in her life?

evening's story, tell your child that you are there to listen. What can he tell you about himself, his day, his plans, fears, or questions? Look him in the eye and listen carefully with an open, loving, and accepting heart.

Figure out a regular time that would best suit you, your schedule, and your family. Just remember, when you listen, you want all of your attention to be focused on your child. Ask questions to more fully understand but withhold your opinion, judgment, or your own similar experiences. You are loving your child by truly listening.

If this is a new framework for interacting with your children, don't be surprised if they don't immediately start talking. They may be expecting that you will share your opinions, thoughts, or assessment. Be patient.

● Reality: we can't make them do what we want

Consider this: When you ask your child to clean his room, were you and he sitting in the same room with him looking intently at you, just waiting for you to make a request? If he was, you are living with an extraordinary child. My guess is that you ask your child to clean his room while he is doing some other activity even though that activity may be unproductive, such as watching television. Your child is occupied and entertained, even if that is not immediately apparent to you. He has plans and ideas of his own. Cleaning his room is probably not on his agenda. This doesn't mean that cleaning his room cannot be put on his agenda; however, it is probably a new idea and agenda item for him.

Most school children beyond first grade know that homework is part of their daily lives. They even know this without your having to remind them. For some children, diving into completing homework is a task they are willing to do or will tolerate doing. For others, this is not true. If this is your situation, when you remind her over and over and over again, your reluctant child is not more willing to do her homework. Usually the result is quite the opposite; now, your child doesn't want to do her homework *and* she doesn't want to be nagged by you.

The parents of a family probably share a quality world picture of what they want their children to want, but this does not mean that their children have the same pictures. Equally true is the fact that just because children have quality world pictures of what they want their parents to want does not mean that parents have the same pictures. Here are some common examples of pictures parents usually share:

● A mother may have a picture in her head that her child will eat all vegetables. Most parents want their children to eat a well-balanced diet.

- A father has a picture that his child will be successful in school. This father believes that his child understands that completing homework is a school responsibility.
- A mother has a quality world picture that her child is a responsible, contributing member of the family. This means that the child will complete chores without complaining or needing to be reminded every day.
- In a father's quality world picture of his child, the child doesn't swear or whine when he is not getting his own way.

All of these ideas and pictures are understandable. They may sound a bit idealistic, naïve, or unrealistic, but that doesn't prevent parents from wanting their children to behave responsibly and wonderfully all of the time. The trouble is that children's behaviors often fall short of their parents' expectations and desires. Even then, you still don't stop wanting what you want.

Using the common practice of rewarding or withdrawing what your child desires may change your child's behavior or manipulate your child into behaving the way you want her to, but the price you pay for such maneuvers is the degradation of the quality of your relationship with your child, at least for a time. Ultimately, rewards and punishments stop working.

The reality is that parents *can't* make their children start or stop doing anything! Luckily, parents do have an enormous capacity to *influence* their children's behavior. This new process of parenting actually enhances your relationship with each other, and the process will help both parent and child to find better ways to fulfill your needs for power—power with each other.

The key to this process is sharing with your child what your quality world picture is—what you want. Ask your child what his quality world picture is—what he wants. Then work together to find a solution that helps you both get most of the picture that you each want.

If I had written this book for children, this chapter would have started like this: How do I get my parents to let me eat only what I want to eat at dinner, which means no vegetables? How do I get my parents to stop nagging me about my homework and chores? How can I get my parents to let me have what I want the first time I ask, instead of waiting until I resort to swearing or whining to get my own way?

Get it? You are behaving in ways intended to change your child and get her to be or do what you want. Your child is behaving in ways she hopes will change you and get you to do or be what she wants. Instead of trying to control each other, work it out. Talk about the quality world pictures you want. Make a plan together so you both get more of what you want—together.

● Are your requests reasonable?

When you ask your child to clean his room or do her homework or come to the dinner table, you know these are not unreasonable requests. Yet it can begin to feel as if everything is becoming an argument, like you are pulling in one direction and your child is pulling in the opposite direction.

However, just as illustrated with the example about the dinner conflict, your children are not sitting idly, doing absolutely nothing except waiting for you to call them for dinner. Just as you have been busy preparing the meal, your children have been busy doing their own activities. When you call them for dinner, they feel like they are being interrupted. If your child is engaged in something fully engrossing, he may be slow or reluctant to drop his activity and move on to dinner. What your child is thinking goes something like this: *Why can't she just wait one moment while I finish this last bit? She is always so insistent that I come as soon as she calls.*

This doesn't mean that your child is more justified in his position than you are in yours. It does mean that your child is no *less* justified. You have been working hard to get the family meal on the table. Your child has been working hard doing something else.

● Enlist your child's help

All this may sound reasonable and understandable, but sometimes you just wish your child would do what you ask because you have asked. Sometimes you wish you didn't have to nag, cajole, and plead to get compliance. You may be beginning to feel tired, and you may also be feeling increasingly unhappy with the nag you realize you are turning into.

Here is a suggestion. Enlist your child's help. Arrange for your interactions with your children to go differently using your powers of prediction and clairvoyance. Choose one issue to begin with. If you want to start with the one that annoys you the most, that's fine. If you want to start with the one that you think you are most likely to be successful with, that will work too. Just choose one.

Then, the next time you and your child are feeling friendly toward each other, approach her. The timing for your approach needs to be well away from the offending time. Often Saturday afternoons or late on Sunday mornings are good times. Whenever it is, it should be a relaxed time with fewer obligations or outside activities. Then tell your child you have something important to discuss with her. For example, tell her you want to discuss piano practice time with her. Explain to her what it would be like if you had a magic wand and could make it happen in an ideal way.

"If daily piano practice time went as I wished, every day you would decide when you were going to practice your piano lesson. Sometimes,

For a three-day holiday, you and your family decide to take a trip to a fun vacation spot. This will entail a long car trip for you, your spouse, your fourteen-year-old son, and your eleven-year-old daughter. Your daughter has plans to watch her portable DVD player when she is bored with scenery watching and to play the license plate game with you. Your son will be plugged into his iPod. But when you stop at a rest stop or to have a meal, you need him to be able to listen and participate in conversation with the rest of the family, not just plug into his iPod and disengage from the family. Which is the best method for working this out?

without me even asking, you would tell me when you have scheduled your practice session. Other days, you might wait until I asked. Then, when that time arrived, you would sit down and play your piano lesson. Later, when television time came in the evening, we could all sit down together, knowing you had completed your piano practice time. We both could relax and enjoy that special evening time."

This is a very specific picture of the ideal daily piano practice time from the mom's point of view.

● Establish a rule stating that listening to iPods or watching DVD players is only allowed in the car, during travel time. Deliver and explain the rule to your son and daughter before you begin the trip.

● Explain to your son that you need and want him to participate and connect with the family during rest stops and eating times. Ask your son if he can create a plan to accommodate your desires.

● Wait and see how the interactions evolve during the trip.

● Explain to your son what you need and want. Ask him what he needs and wants. Ask him to help you make a plan to accommodate both perspectives.

Each of the above options will work, but the last one is probably the best way to help you all get more of what you want without assuming your wishes should take highest priority simply because you are the parent. If you work this out as you are planning the trip, well before the travel begins, you will have greater chances of success and a much more enjoyable trip.

Next, ask your child to describe to you what her picture is for ideal piano practice time. She may start with, "If it was ideal, I wouldn't have to practice my piano lessons. If it was perfect I would just know how to play the piano magically," but don't let that discourage you. You may need to remind her that the way to get to perfect piano playing is through daily practice. Stick with it and ask her to describe her ideal daily piano practice sessions. As she describes her quality world pictures to you, do your best to have her get into the details of the picture. What time of day is it? Are there people in the room with her? Is she practicing her scales and skills first or working on the assigned piece of music? Is she drinking anything? Completely accept her description fully.

Using your quality picture and your daughter's quality picture, together work out a plan where you both will get some of what you want. Plan for success; then evaluate after attempting to implement the plan. Keep planning, implementing, evaluating, and replanning until you are successful together.

● Setting limits

This peaceful parenting process is not permissive parenting. Just because you understand that you cannot control your children's behavior does not mean that whatever a child does is acceptable. You are still obligated to set standards and limits for your children.

In fact, understanding why there is a need to set limits and standards for your children is an important part of understanding this parenting process. Children are born with a genetic drive for freedom, but this does not mean there are no limits. Your job is to establish boundaries, allowing only as much freedom as a child has responsible behaviors to handle. As you increase your children's freedom, you must teach them the additional responsible behaviors necessary for handling the additional freedom. You must set standards and set limits.

The distinction between this parenting process and other kinds of parenting programs does not lie in the kinds of standards and limits set. The distinction is how we manage ourselves and our children when our children do not meet our standards or abide by our limits.

Conventional wisdom teaches adults to use external control to ensure that children will meet standards and abide by limits. If a child does not do his homework, many parents either punish the child by

parenting tip

D o you have trouble getting the family to the table for dinner? Dinnertime will go more smoothly if you give your family ample warning before dinner is ready. Give everyone a fifteen-minute warning, then a ten-minute warning, then a five-minute warning. Arrange a rotatable schedule so that your children are helping you set the table and clean up afterward. You might also include a chef's helper position as another rotating job. Including your children in meal preparation, setting the table, and cleaning up for this vital family event will increase the likelihood that your children will show up for the meal on time.

taking away some privilege or threaten to do so. For example if a child does not follow the limits of his curfew, many parents take away the child's privilege of going out the next time.

When you adopt this peaceful parenting process, you can still expect that your children will complete their piano practice sessions. You can still set a curfew when your children leave the house. However, if your child fails to complete her piano practice session or does not comply with the agreed-upon curfew, you do not attempt to externally control your child. Parents who use this process work with their children on meeting expectations and limits without resorting to threats, punishments, or other forms of external control.

Giving up the urge to externally control your children into compliance is difficult because you have pictures in your quality world that show your children meeting your expectations. When they don't, you still feel the urge to get your children to do what you want. The difference is that with this improved parenting knowledge, you understand that trying to externally control your children is not the answer.

But what can a parent who uses this process do? It is very difficult to change your parenting habits, so here are some interim steps to help you get started.

Step 1: Set the limit or standard. Explain to your child why you have set the limit or standard that you have given her. Whenever possible, ask for your child's opinion and incorporate her ideas into a compromise limit or standard.

Step 2: Expect compliance. Explain to your child what your standard or limit is or reiterate what you have agreed upon. Ask if he understands the standard or limit and is willing to abide by it. State that you expect him to comply.

Step 3: Make a plan ahead of time for possible noncompliance. Talk with your child about how the two of you should work out a conflict in case she doesn't respect the limit or meet the standard. Ask her how she wants you to handle this possibility. Explain that you want to avoid punishments, threats, or imposing any kind of consequence. Explain that your goal is to work together to reach success.

Step 4: Work things out together if your child doesn't meet the standard or comply with the limit. Based on the plan you agreed upon in step 3, follow the plan of talking together. Using the magical question, ask your child what he wanted that he tried to get by not meeting the standard or abiding by the limit. Work together to come up with a new standard or limit that incorporates your child's desire responsibly. This may mean that you need to alter your expectation or limit slightly.

Step 5: *Don't give up.* Continue following steps 1–4 until you and your child have worked together successfully and found a mutually agreed-upon limit or standard. This is the most important step of all. When you continue to work with your child on this issue, she will know that you mean business and are not going to give up until you reach success together. She may be accustomed to your usual attempts at externally controlling her. She is given her punishment, takes it, and still eventually gets what she wants. Most children know that parents will not persist for long enough. Children "win" because of their parents' lack of staying power. In this peaceful parenting process you and your child both win because you work together to figure out how you both can get what you want.

● Unsolicited advice

As a parent, you want to help your children learn as much as possible, and succeed in all they do so they can become the best they can be. But sometimes your help is interpreted by your children as anything but helpful. Your own memories may help you understand this idea.

If you've been pregnant, think back to that time. Were you forced to listen to all of the horror stories pertaining to pregnancy and delivery from every mother you encountered? Did your mother, mother-in-law, aunt, cousin, and godmother each give you her best advice about what you should and should not do?

When you went out with your infant, did the advice continue? During a grocery store outing when your baby or toddler began a tantrum, did total strangers feel compelled to give you "good" advice? Now that your child or children are older, does every casual question you ask of another parent elicit a lecture that leaves you feeling less competent or less able to handle your problem than before you brought it up?

We can also approach this from another angle. Are *you* the person who is sharing your good ideas and tips with other parents who have children younger than your own? It's hard not to. We each have our own stories, our own experiences, our own wisdom learned from lessons our children present to us. How can we resist teaching another mother what we have learned from our own parenting experiences?

Sometimes the advice we receive from others is welcome. Sometimes the tip your mother-in-law or older sister shares about walking with a cranky infant is just the method that finally helps you and your baby settle down. Learning the trick about laying your toddler's jacket on the ground for her to climb into might be the perfect advice for motivating your daughter to learn how to dress herself. Another mother's advice about her son's bedtime ritual might be the ticket to help you and your son find peace and success at bedtime.

But sometimes advice, no matter how well intentioned, feels like criticism. When your mother suggests that you hug your child more, you wonder if you are unloving. When your daughter's teacher suggests that you spend more time helping her with her homework, you begin to worry that you are less involved than you should be.

What makes the difference between helpful advice or well-meant suggestions and criticism? The biggest difference is whether or not you have asked for help and advice. When you ask your sister-in-law how she handles the bickering between her two children, you want her to share her experiences, hoping to learn some tricks to solve your problem. But when a total stranger suggests you hold your son's hand while walking through the department store, the advice feels like someone else has evaluated what you are doing and decided it is not okay. You haven't asked for, nor are you ready to receive, any parenting ideas, thank you very much, so when unsolicited advice is offered, it is more likely to be perceived as unhelpful. When you solicit advice, you are open to helpful suggestions for handling a challenge or problem that you have acknowledged exists.

Now take a moment to imagine what life is like from your child's perspective. Almost every place in your child's life is populated by an older person at the ready to offer advice, suggestions for improvement, or correction. At home, one or both parents expresses ideas about how your son could manage his time better. At school, your daughter's teacher hands back work with corrections. At music lessons or on the softball or baseball field, the teacher or coach may yell at your son in an effort to help him improve his skills. The life of a child is filled with unsolicited advice and corrections from every angle and from unlimited sources.

When is advice and correction helpful to your child and when is it a threat to her self-esteem? Just as with you, the difference is determined by whether or not the advice or correction has been asked for.

When your son is making his bed and has trouble tucking in or fitting the sheet, if he asks for your help or suggestions, he wants advice. But if you happen to walk by at his moment of struggle and suggest that tucking in corner angles first may help, your suggestion may easily be perceived as criticism.

When your daughter asks her coach what she can do to improve her basketball skills, she wants advice and help. But when the coach tells her that she was in the wrong place for the last play, your daughter may leave the court questioning her skills and abilities.

It would be grand if from this day forward you completely eliminated giving all unsolicited advice, to your children and all of the other people in your life. That would be my unsolicited advice to you. But until I can succeed at such a feat myself, I won't offer it to you.

Instead, here's a piece of advice you can really use. *Ask.* It truly is that simple. When you see your daughter struggling with her homework, ask her if she would like your help. When you hear your son mistakenly name the capital of South Dakota, ask if he would like your advice. When you see another mother juggling her baby, carriage, and dog, ask if you can help. Your attempt to help, to correct, to offer your hard-earned wisdom will be more readily accepted if you first ask if the person wants to receive your ideas, advice, and suggestions.

● Conclusion

Even though your wishes to have your children comply with your every request and demand seem reasonable to you, the error in that thinking is probably clear to you now. If you want your children to mature into independent thinkers who take personal responsibility for their actions, these skills must first be learned at home with you. Setting limits and offering help when your children have asked for this advice are steps you can take to help your children learn these skills. Although it is challenging to think of your children as the potential mature and independent people they will become, the more you can aim in that direction, the better the outcome will be for you and your children.

parenting
Q&A

Q *My twelve-year-old stepdaughter is an enthusiastic soccer player. She plays on a competitive traveling team. This year her new coach seems to have an approach toward the game that is very different from her previous coaches. He seems to spend a great deal of time yelling at the girls and berating them. My stepdaughter believes that this is just the coach's style. She thinks that he gets carried away by his desire to win and that he works hard so the team will be the best. I'm concerned that he is too mean. Will he hurt my child's feelings and diminish her love of the game? I am tempted to take my stepdaughter off this team altogether, but anytime I mention this, she becomes angry and upset. Is there a peaceful way that I can handle this problem?*

A Leave your stepdaughter on this team. Believe her when she tells you that she does not feel hurt or diminished. You are observing the potentially hurtful and harmful behaviors, but there must be more going ▶

parenting

Q&A

on than you know, otherwise, your stepdaughter would not be able to overlook this coach's style and defend him.

Unsolicited advice can present potential difficulties. How-ever, when an expert whom we respect offers us feedback, and we believe that this person has our best interest at heart, we hear his words as suggestions to help us improve. In other words, your stepdaughter sees this coach as a person who is interested in helping her and her team to be the best that they can be. Because she believes this, she hears his words and his delivery style as helpful instructions and information from an expert that she can use to improve her soccer skills.

This coach probably has other kinds of interactions and exchanges with the girls on the team. If all the coach ever did was criticize, berate, yell, and belittle, no girls would want to be around him or do their best, including your stepdaughter. The time the team spends together encompasses practices, drilling, strategic planning, after-game discussions, pregame talks, and more. You are not privy to all of these interactions. Kind words and connections are probably there, but outside of your observations.

No parent wants to watch as a person of influence and authority seemingly mistreats her child. But your stepdaughter is telling you that this is not the case here. To overrule her decision would be an injustice. Her evaluation is that this coach is not doing her harm.

However, you don't need to sit idly by, hoping for the best. Continue to talk to your stepdaughter about her coach and soccer. Get curious and find out why she likes this coach. What is she learning from him about herself and about soccer? Find out if and when the good times exist between this coach and the team. Stay involved, but then trust that your daughter is strong enough in her belief in herself and her soccer abilities that this coach's style will not destroy her love for the sport.

5.

Fun

Your secret weapon

The mother of a kindergarten child told me this story about how her family dealt with a difficult situation. Unfortunately, her daughter was in morning kindergarten. The reason this was unfortunate was that this little girl was not a morning person. Her mother would enter her daughter's bedroom each morning and brightly tell her daughter it was time to get up and get dressed to begin another wonderful day. Her daughter did not see the magic in getting up early, so she would roll over and ignore the mother's request. After asking, nagging, and finally resorting to yelling, this mom was able to get her daughter out of bed, but starting each morning with this routine was unpleasant for both mother and child. Her husband suggested that he might be able to help. He was not a morning person either, but he thought he could find an intriguing game that would help their daughter get out of bed more easily in the morning.

The first morning, the mom watched as her husband entered their daughter's room and began to sing morning reveille. "Time to get up, time to get up, time to get up this morning. What shall we wear, what shall we wear, what shall we wear this morning?" The mom was amazed to see her daughter sit up in bed, stretch, and smile at her father. This went on each day, progressing further into the game until finally one day the mother walked in to see her husband and daughter dancing and singing as they began the day.

● Children need fun

Children have a huge need for fun. This is something all adults and parents already know. We can't keep children from having fun. Watch a child during a church service. This creative bundle of energy will do all sorts of things to entertain and have fun. First he will swing his legs back and forth, getting everyone in his pew to start rocking back and forth until finally an adult places a hand on the child to stop the leg swinging. Next he will pick up the hymnal, open it, and turn it upside down, attempting to read the words that way. As he tries to pronounce the words aloud, his parent again touches him to signal him to stop. Finally, he begins counting the number of freckles on the bald head of the fellow sitting in front of him. Again, the adult will grab hold of his pointing finger and place it back into the child's lap.

We have all experienced times when our children are bound and determined to have fun no matter how inappropriate the place or circumstances. But this is valuable information for us. Knowing that our children have such a boundless need for fun, we can increase the chances that our children will do what we ask them to do if we can insert play into the request or chore.

parenting tip

 I f you have a child who is a "challenging eater," you may like this tip from Brenda, mother of five-year-old Brianna. "Brianna stopped eating when she was two. I was quite concerned. Then Brianna and I discovered a game together. Here's how it goes.

"I fill Brianna's plate with food. Sitting next to her, I cover my eyes as she chooses something from the plate to put in her mouth. As she begins chewing, I try to guess what she is eating.

"'It sounds crunchy,' I say. Or 'That sounds like something green. Are you eating a frog?' What I say is less important than saying something that causes her to feel as though she is fooling me. The guessing game becomes so much fun for her that she doesn't even notice that she is eating. This ended the struggle over eating and food."

Instead of simply requesting that your children put their seat belts on as you get into the car together, turn this necessary safety habit into a family sporting event. The first person to buckle up wins the gold, the second the silver, and the third the bronze medal. Once they discover that there is status for the winner of this sport, your children will scramble to get their seat belts fastened.

● Let your child show you how

Our children are actually our teachers who remind us about our own basic need and instinct for fun. Children never forget to laugh and play. Unfortunately, as adults we too often get caught up in our responsibilities and jobs. If we follow our children's lead, we can spend less time saying, "Playtime is over. Now we need to get to work." We can change this to "That's enough of the hard work. We need to laugh and play more!"

When you were a child were you told, "You can go out and play after you get your work done"? As a child, how much work did you need to do? Was it possible to complete your work and still find time to play? Probably. However, you may still be living by this same rule. If you are, when will you ever get your work done so that you can play? Probably never!

You may be thinking that all of this sounds good, but you are not clever enough to create a game for the various tasks you are asking your child to complete. But here's the beauty of this idea. You don't have to come up with the ideas! You're living with an expert. Your child knows how to turn anything and everything into a game, remember? So instead of wondering and worrying how to turn emptying the dishwasher, taking out the garbage, or carrying laundry down to the laundry room into some kind of game, simply ask your child to figure out a game. Don't be surprised when she comes up with a very clever idea. Depending on your child's age, she may come up with a very convoluted and complicated game with many rules. Again, don't worry about trying to keep track of it all—your child can do that. Remember, she also has a need for power, so she will like being in charge of the rules and noticing times when you break the rules.

One mother asked her two-year-old to carry a package for her while they were out shopping.

"No," he said. "I don't want to."

"Can you carry the package on your head?" she asked.

He grabbed the package and proudly showed her how he could. When she asked him if he was having fun carrying the package on his head, he quickly corrected her and told her how powerful, strong, and proud he felt.

● Don't pit siblings against each other

When Paul and David were preschoolers our family would some-times go out in the evening. My children were up at the crack of dawn no matter how late they went to bed the night before; however, if my children didn't have a solid eight hours of sleep, the next day would find them cranky, whiny, and less cooperative with me and with each other. Knowing this, I always wanted them to get into their pajamas, brush their teeth, and get into bed as quickly as possible after our late night out. But no matter how much I asked, cajoled, nagged, or yelled, I couldn't seem to speed up the pace of their bedtime preparations.

One evening I found the key to success. Just as we pulled into the driveway, I challenged the boys with a game. "Let's see who can get into bed first, the two of you or me. We have to have our pajamas on, our teeth brushed, and be in bed first in order to win. Go!"

At that point Paul and David both ran into the house, ran up the stairs, took off their clothes, put on their pajamas, brushed their teeth, and were in bed first. The two of them had won! And this is when I dis-covered that turning my requests and desires into a game increased the chances that the boys could get what they wanted and so could I. They wanted to play and have fun. I wanted them in bed quickly. Turning my desire into a game where they could play and I could get them in bed quickly meant we all got what we wanted.

Notice that the boys were competing against me, not each other.

peaceful parenting quiz

M ake a list of all of your chores that you find tedious or odious. Ask your children to do the same for their own chores, homework drills, and so on. Now ask each person to come up with ideas for making the job into a game. Here are some ideas to get you started.

- Complete the job while blindfolded.
- Complete the job while hopping on one foot.
- Ask one person to provide the play-by-play color description of another person's actions while she does the chore, as if describing a televised sporting event.
- Share the job, while taking turns singing and guessing the titles of various songs.
- Ask the children to do your work while you do theirs for a day.

Which idea did you like best? Which idea did each child like best? Which ideas are you willing to try out?

Avoid creating games that pit siblings against one another. As you are probably already aware, children are competing with each other all of the time anyway. To encourage or increase this tendency by creating competitive games will not be helpful to you or at least one child. Instead, ask the children to become a team that competes against the adults in the house. This encourages them to work together and cooperate with each other. This they will love!

● Will teenagers play along?

One clever mother helped her daughter see her daily chore as a different kind of game. The teenager's daily job was to scoop their dog's poop from the fenced-in backyard. Instead of simply asking her daughter to complete the task, this mom would stand and watch as her daughter scooped and tossed the dog's business to a designated area. Her rating was determined by how close to the spot the toss landed. "That was an 8.5," her mother would declare after one toss. "Only a 3 for that one," might be another rating. Or, "Yes, you hit the spot. That was a 10!" her mother would proclaim. Do you see how differently this chore was viewed by her daughter because her mother helped her change an unpleasant job into folly and fun?

If you, too, are the parent of teenagers, be prepared for them to scowl and deny that anything you want to do will be fun. One way that adolescents have fun is to let you know that you, their parent, are no fun! "That's really dumb" or "I'm not doing that stupid idea" are the typical responses you will receive when you suggest to your teenager that you play a game together as you fold laundry. But despite their words, often they will participate, telling you years later how much they enjoyed playing your "stupid" games. Don't let their words discourage your use of this secret weapon.

parenting tip

 Ugh! It's the end of the day and your children are complaining because they don't want to clean up the huge mess they themselves have created. You don't want to either. Here is one solution that might help:

Clever Clean-Up Game. You'll need several medium-sized toy boxes; several medium-sized toy bins; several large, soft cloth bags; and bookshelves or a bookcase. Alternately, you use the toy storage system you already have.

Before cleanup begins, ask one child to guess the number of stuffed animals he thinks will fit into one of the soft bags. Together, count how many actually fit as you place them into the bag. See how close the guess was to the final number.

Repeat this process, guessing the number of toys with wheels that will fit into one toy box, the number of books that one shelf will hold, the number of toys with the color red on them that will fit into a bin, and so on.

Create as many variations as you can think of; then ask your children to come up with as many categories as they can think of.

Hint: If you have more than one child, don't have them compete against each other as this will result in arguments and sulking. Instead, have the children compete against themselves and their own guessed number.

● Rule review

Summertime is a perfect time for you and your children to maximize fun. Chances are your lives are less structured during this season, leaving more opportunity for spontaneous fun activities. Revising and reviewing the family rules, including bedtime, keeps these moments fun while decreasing confusion and disappointment.

First, decide as parents if you would like to include some new freedoms you feel your children now are able to handle that should be reflected in the family rules. For instance, can bedtimes be changed? Second, decide if there are different kinds of chores that need attending to during the summer months, like mowing the lawn, weeding the garden, or watering the flower beds. Is one of your children old enough and able to begin handling the lawn mower? Once you, the parents, have decided how you would like the family to function during the summer, it is time for a family discussion that includes the children.

Plan a family meeting at the very beginning of summer vacation. Share with your children the nonnegotiable rules—like violin practice or chores that will continue during the summer. Explain to your children what these rules are and why they are in place. If your children complain about them or want to change them, at least listen to their arguments. Then decide if there is indeed room for negotiation.

Next, suggest the change of rules that you want to put on the table for negotiation. For instance, if you are willing to change the children's bedtime, explain that you are willing to negotiate this rule. Ask your children if they are interested in the change as well. What time do they think would be reasonable? What time were you thinking of? Then work together to decide on a new bedtime. Follow this same procedure for all of the additional changes you have considered before your meeting. Ask the children if they have any changes or rules they want that you have not brought into the discussion.

Be sure you set a time for when you will have another family meeting. At this next meeting, review the new rules and evaluate your success and discuss whether you need to clarify or modify the rules. Additional issues may also have arisen that you had not anticipated at your initial meeting. Bring these issues into the conversation and establish reasonable and mutually satisfying rules.

For instance, one summer following Paul and David's seventh-grade year, they left the house at nine o'clock in the morning and did not check in with me until after three o'clock that afternoon. Although this had been their schedule when they were in school, it was not acceptable to me during summer vacation. I was not sure where they had been all day. We discussed the situation and created a rule that stipulated that they would check in with me at lunchtime, either by coming home for lunch or calling me to let me know where they were. I had not anticipated the need for this rule at the beginning of summer vacation during our first family meeting about the summer rules. You may have similar experiences.

Taking the time to revise and review rules at the beginning of the summer will help the whole family enjoy the fun of summer more completely. Because you are all clear with each other about what is expected, together you will have greater harmony and peace during this wonderful time of the year.

● Conclusion

Of course not everything you ask your children to do must be fun. It is reasonable to expect that your children will participate in daily chores and activities even when the job is not fun. But changing tedium into fun enhances everyone's life! Many women who consider regularly cleaning the house to be part of their job, like to clean with music blasting. They dance and sing as they work. At the end of the job they never say, "That was so much fun, I think I'll do it again," but finding some way to change this tedious chore into a more enjoyable one enhances the activity.

This is a chance to learn from your children and use their inherent secret weapon to increase the joy, pleasure, laughter, and cooperation in your family. Make playing and laughing a priority and a family tradition that your children will pass on to their children!

parenting

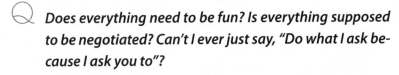

Q *Does everything need to be fun? Is everything supposed to be negotiated? Can't I ever just say, "Do what I ask because I ask you to"?*

A The simple answer to your question is no, you do not need to turn every chore into fun and games. When you ask your child to follow a direction, you don't need to negotiate every time. You certainly have the right to expect that your child will do as you ask, when you ask, simply because you have asked. This is respectful, courteous behavior.

Similarly, you also complete necessary child-care chores without having them all become fun and games. I hope that sometimes you fulfill simple requests your child makes simply because he has made them. You are setting the example, teaching him how people who respect and love one another treat one another.

Turning dreary tasks into fun and games means you understand that your child has the inherent need for fun. When and if you make chores and tasks more fun, it increases the likelihood that your child will complete the chore or task without complaint. Children can't resist fun! But they can resist tasks and chores. Not everything must be fun, but if you can increase the fun involved in daily living, both you and your child will be more satisfied while following your inherent drives.

If every time your daughter resisted your request, she demanded to negotiate and you agreed, you would soon be exhausted! If every time you and your son had a dispute, he got his way and you didn't, your need for power would be thwarted. The same is true from your children's point of view. If every time you and your daughter disagreed, you got your way and she didn't, her need for power would never be satisfied.

Negotiations are helpful when you and your child have two different pictures. Working together, you can try to negotiate a way for both of you to get some of what you want. Or sometimes negotiation can lead you both to a completely new solution, a new quality world picture. Thus both of you meet your need for power with one another.

You don't have to go through this process every time there is a conflict. Rather, do a bit of self-evaluation. How often are you letting your child win? How often are you winning? What requests seem to be turning into battles over who will win? These are the areas that need to be considered as points of negotiation.

6.

Allowing them to do it alone

My eight-year-old son isn't willing to help me with household chores anymore. In the past he was so enthusiastic about each job. Now when I ask him, he simply refuses in a dull and subdued way." This question was asked of me by a father attending one of my parenting lectures.

When children reach this age, they often become less enthusiastic about helping with various household chores. Children grow sophisticated enough to realize that these chores are work, not play. Washing dishes isn't about playing in soap bubbles, for example. Making the bed is not an excuse to throw pillows into the air and flop onto the bed.

"You're not going back and redoing his completed chores, are you?" I asked him, innocently.

"Well, yes, I am," he admitted sheepishly. "He's so young and small that he isn't able to do an adequate job."

"There is no doubt in my mind that you, a thirty-two-year-old man, can more adequately and competently make a bed, dust a room, or fold laundry than your eight-year-old son can. But if every time you ask your son to complete a chore, you go in and improve upon his accomplishments, what message do you think your son is receiving?"

This father understood perfectly without me having to explain further. But lowering some of your standards and allowing your children to do jobs for themselves is easier said than done. Sometimes you help your children because there doesn't seem to be enough time. See if this scene seems familiar to you.

It's a school morning, and unfortunately you awaken forty-five minutes late. Horrors! Already it's a bad day and the day has just begun. If you are forty-five minutes late, then everybody else is too. You quickly get your children out of bed, throwing some clothes in their direction, gathering and throwing breakfast in their direction too. You let the dog in and out several times while you answer a few important e-mails that you have to reply to this morning.

While you are gathering up the library books that are due today, you keep an eye on your children and realize that they are moving remarkably efficiently too. Finally, you sign the permission slip that must be returned to your daughter's teacher today. You tell your children that this morning you will give them a ride to school because there isn't enough time to catch the school bus, you grab your son's sneakers to help him put them on, and you herd everybody toward the door. You're still going to be late, but not as late as you had initially feared.

"Put your shoes on, honey, and let Mommy tie them so we can get going," you say.

"But Mommy, I want to tie them myself," he tells you proudly.

Uh-oh, you know what this means. Your son is in the beginning stages of learning to tie his shoes. This is a complicated motor skill. If you allow your son to accomplish this task himself, you know it will take another forty-five minutes. So what do you do? Here are some choices:

Plan A: Choose a different pair of sneakers and tell him, "It's a Velcro day today, honey!"

Plan B: Pick your child up and put him in the car with his sneakers. Tell him to do the best he can to tie his shoes between your house and school. When you arrive at school, you finish whatever he hasn't successfully completed on his own and send him on his way.

Plan C: Pick your child up and put him in the car with his sneakers. Tell him to do the best he can to tie his shoes between your house and school. If he hasn't completed the job by the time you've arrived at school, pick him up again and deliver him to his classroom and teacher. Explain to the teacher that he is learning to tie his own shoes and is now practicing. Wish them all a pleasant day and leave.

Plan D: When your child declares that he wants to tie his shoes himself, smile and say, "Okay, honey. Go ahead." Take advantage of this breather. Prepare yourself a second cup of coffee and sit with your son as he proudly practices his new skill. You are already late. What difference is it going to make if you are a few minutes later?

Even though it may seem that the last plan is intended to be the best answer, that is not true. Each one of these choices is good and reasonable.

● The unspoken message

The question you need to ask yourself is, *How often do I do things for my child or with my child and how often do I allow her to do things on her own?*

Every time your child attempts to do something new—whether that is tying a shoelace, completing a science project, baking a batch of cookies, making a bed, or driving a car—if you intervene and do the task for her, pretty soon she is going to stop even attempting the task. Why should she try? Since her parent jumps in and takes over every time she attempts this job, the child begins to understand the unspoken message: her abilities and swiftness are not as good as her parent's.

The other unspoken message that parents may convey, whether they intend to or not, is that nothing less than perfection is acceptable. Is this what you intend to communicate? Probably not.

Pay attention to all the times you allow your child to practice his new skill, task, or chore on his own. Accept that each new skill is going

parenting tip

Report cards are often a source of conflict between parents and children. Instead of resorting to the same old "blame game," try this strategy. It worked well for Robert and his parents. When he brought home a bad report card in the fourth grade, they didn't get angry or upset with him. They ignored all the excuse making and blaming that Robert was doing. Instead, they asked him how he felt about his report card. Was he satisfied? Did he think he could do better?

Then they told him that his schoolwork was now going to be his responsibility. They were interested in helping, but he needed to ask for their help. They told him that if he could clearly describe what to take more time initially. Accept that the quality of the work will be less than what you can do yourself—but not forever, just for now as your child is learning.

● What's the hurry?

A father of a two-year-old complained that these suggestions are too time consuming. When his daughter fails to follow his instructions to go directly to the car to be buckled into her car seat to start the day, he can't imagine taking the extra time to get into a conversation about it with his daughter. Instead, this father finds it quicker to pick his daughter up and put her in the car seat. What follows is our dialogue.

they could do that would be helpful to him, they would gladly oblige.

As hard as it was, when they saw Robert playing computer games or watching television before he had finished his school-work, they said nothing. The more they backed off, the more likely he was to ask for specific help. Every few days during a family meal, they would ask Robert if he needed any help. Some of those times he did ask for help. Other times he declined their offer.

Although the beginning was rocky, by the end of the school year Robert had raised all of his grades to As or Bs. They all stopped haggling, arguing, and getting upset over schoolwork. Schoolwork is Robert's job and responsibility. His parents care and he knows it. But even more importantly, they know now that Robert cares too.

"When you pick your daughter up and put her in her car seat, does this work? Are you always successful?"

"Yes," he answered.

"Have you had the experience where you attempt to pick your daughter up and she makes this maneuver difficult?"

"Well, sure, that happens sometimes too."

"Have you had the experience where you attempt to put your daughter into her car seat but she goes rigid on you, refusing to bend and sit in her car seat? Does it ever begin to feel like a battle?"

Again, he admitted that he had experienced these incidents too.

"And how much time have you saved when you had that kind of an experience? Let me also ask you, how did you feel during and after those upsets between you and your daughter?"

Who ever said that our job of parenting was a quick and easy one? Are you searching for some ideas that will make your job easier and faster? If you take the time to search long enough, you may find those answers. But if you also want the answers to include information on how to parent well, then you are never going to find those answers.

It's true that if you decide to move in the direction of parenting more peacefully, parenting will require more time initially, not less. Every time your two-year-old misbehaves, it takes more time to engage in a conversation and ask him, "What did you want that you were trying to get by grabbing that toy from your sister? If we can figure out a way to help you get the toy and let your sister have a turn with that toy too, are you interested in working it out?"

The alternative method of scolding your child is certainly faster. "Give that back to your sister! You know we don't grab toys from one another in our family" takes longer to type than to carry out. But what is your goal? Are you interested in being an efficient parent today or a parent who helps your child learn to be responsible and independent without you in the long run?

It does feel like working this out with a two-year-old takes too long. But what are you gaining and what are you losing by trying to rush life events along? If you get into the car a little bit more quickly this morning or drop your child off at day care exactly on time today so that you beat the traffic and get to work early, you may have saved time. What damage might you have done to your relationship with your child to gain these few minutes? Are you willing to run the risk of hurting your toddler's feelings simply to gain some more time for work?

Here's a different question. From what other areas in your life can you gain time in your day, week, or life rather than sacrificing your relationship with your child? What else are you doing that is more important than your parenting job? What other relationship is more important? Of course you lead a busy life, but can you structure your life to be less busy without stealing your child's time? Your child does not have the ability to change this. He did not ask to have parents who feel overextended and overcommitted. He does require your time and care. That is the obligation and deal you agreed to with this child when you adopted him or brought him into this world.

Many years ago, Erma Bombeck wrote a very clever and funny column. (From the 1960s to the 1990s Bombeck wrote a newspaper column about the humorous side of being a housewife and mother.) In one particular column she asked her readers to imagine treating their children like their guests or friends and imagine treating their guests like they do their children. Just imagine yelling at your guests who arrive late at your home. Imagine visiting a friend's home and complaining that she never keeps her house clean. Think of accusing your best friend of getting sick on purpose, just to get out of going on a planned outing.

Now imagine, she wrote, that when your children come home from school you greet them at the door with a big smile, a hug, and a kiss, and you offer to hang up their coats and take care of their backpacks. If you treated your child as your special company who asked to stay awake past her bedtime, you would probably agree without hesitation and maybe offer her a favorite snack as a treat. This imagining can go on and on.

The point that Bombeck was making is that we tend to treat our children very differently from our company. In fact, not only is the treatment different, but the attention our friends receive could easily be interpreted as kinder, more loving, and more nurturing. What's wrong with this picture? Who needs our love, support, caring, and kindness more, our children or our friends?

But why make it a contest? Wouldn't it be marvelous to treat both with loving-kindness and care? Parents don't complain that their friends take too much of their time. Have you ever heard of someone asking for tips or hints on how to develop and maintain a friendship more quickly, without so much time and effort? Why would we assume that living, loving, and guiding our children should be any less time consuming?

● Helping children help themselves

"Amy is going to do fine in college," Carl, the father of eighteen-year-old twins tells me. "I knew she would. All through school she has been well organized and hardworking. With her, I never had to ask, 'Do you have any homework?' or 'Do you need help?' But with Andrew it's different. I'd ask if he did his homework. If he said yes, I knew I needed to see it. He needed help organizing. I had to explain the directions more than once and then stay on him to complete his work. Now that he is in college, I fear he is drowning. He didn't even tell me how much trouble he was in until I finally pulled it out of him. I just don't know how he's going to make it in school."

Was this situation an example of the effects of nature or nurture? Was Andrew a child born with more difficulties organizing, managing, and completing his work? Asking this father for more information gave me clues.

"You tell me that Andrew is going to a culinary college. Why did he choose that kind of school?"

"Oh, he loves to cook. He has always loved to cook, and he is amazing. This has been his passion since he was a little boy."

"So when he did all of this cooking and baking at home, was he able to organize the menu, gather the ingredients, and manage his time so that dishes were prepared to arrive at the table at the same time?" I asked.

"Oh, yes. It's the academics that he struggles with."

If Andrew is able to demonstrate the skills of organizing, managing, and following through in one area, then his academic problems are probably not genetic or due to nature. There may be two factors at play here.

First, if Andrew never learned how to transfer these important skills into the area of academics, it seems that now will be a time for him to learn. As his father points out, in areas of his life where his interests and passions were strong, he demonstrated success. Now he may need assistance in learning how to transfer the skills he uses in the kitchen to school assignments, reports, and exam study.

The second factor involved is that Andrew's dad may have decreased his success by doing work and organizing for him so he never learned how to do these tasks himself. His intention was not to keep his child handicapped and dependent on him. He was attempting to help his child be successful. But as he continued to assist his son, his son never learned how to accomplish these academic skills on his own. Now that the young man is six hundred miles from home, he must do things alone. His father cannot help. Because he never learned, the father's good intentions have brought about very different results from what he wanted.

Your eleven-year-old daughter continues to leave her jacket on the back of a dining room chair instead of putting it on a hanger in the coat closet. Which is the best solution to this problem?

- After asking her once, complete the task yourself.
- After asking her once, hide the jacket from her so she will listen and follow your direction next time.
- After asking her once, collect her from playing her video game and supervise her completion of the task.
- After asking her once, ask her later at dinnertime what you can do to help her remember and complete the task.

See if you have a better idea which solution is the best after reading the next section on nagging.

● How much do you do for your child?

What can Carl and Andrew teach you? Start by listing the tasks that you currently do *for* your children that bring you satisfaction. Which tasks make you say to yourself, *I feel like I'm being a good mother or father when I do this?* As you perform certain functions for your children, are you imagining how happy they will feel? Are there some activities that you automatically assume a parent should do for his child? Take your time in compiling this list. Although you may begin now, keep this list handy as you are reading this book so that you can add to it during the next few days or weeks.

Once the list is made, carefully examine it. What are you now doing for your child that your child could do herself? Of these tasks, are there any you would prefer to stop doing? Are there any on the list that your child has asked to take over? When you are ready, begin by turning one task over to your child. You will probably increase your odds for success if you include your child in the decision about what it is that she will now do instead of you.

● Nagging

"Will you please set the table for dinner?" you ask your child.
No response.
"Will you please set the table for dinner?" you repeat a few minutes later.
No response.
"Will you please set the table?" you ask again a few minutes later.
No response.
Finally, you scream, "Set the table *now*! I've asked you and asked you and I'm not going to ask again!"
"I'll be there in a minute!" your child yells to you from the other room.
Eventually, he shows up and asks you what needs to go on the table, even though this is a chore he has done at least a hundred times before.
If you have made the same request three times in a row, your child has heard you. Continuing to ask becomes nagging. Not only does nagging not help your child complete the requested chore, it also

parenting tip

Back Words Game. We all make mistakes. Children make mistakes frequently. To help them realize that mistakes are okay, easily forgotten, and sometimes even fun and funny, the Back Words Game can help. In this game you say everything backwards. Here are some ideas to get you started:

- Say the alphabet backwards.
- Say individual words backwards.
- Say a sentence backward. For example, "Day nice a having you are?"
- Choose road signs and read them backwards.
- Spell words backwards.

This game is particularly fun during road trips. My nieces have gotten really good at it!

diminishes the quality of your relationship with your child. After all, who wants to spend time with a nag?

Let's look at this from another point of view.

"Mom, can I stay up late tonight?" your child asks.

"No, it's a school night," you reply.

"Please, can I stay up late tonight?" your child asks again.

"No," you answer.

"Please, Mom. Please, please, *please,* can I stay up late tonight?"

Do you think your child is going to change your mind by continuing to ask, to nag, and to beg? If you can be influenced this way, then it's no wonder that your child continues to nag and plead. If you don't change your mind no matter how many times your child asks, nagging only serves to annoy you and erode your feelings of love toward your child, at least at that moment.

Nagging is not helpful behavior and it is not effective. What can you do instead? Before making a request, take time to be clear in your own mind about what you want. Then make the request of your child in a simple and precise way. State what you want and that you need help. Ask your child how you can solicit her help without becoming a nag. Listen to her answer. Ask what your next step should be if your child does not help when you ask. In other words, ask your child to help you learn what to do to avoid nagging. Often, setting a time frame and a time limit can be helpful.

You can also practice this skill in reverse, when your child is nagging you. He makes a request to stay up beyond his bedtime, for example. Ask him why he wants to do that. Explain to him what you want, which is for him to have enough rest and sleep to get up and enjoy the next day. See if together you can find a solution that allows you both to get what you want. Explain that if you can't find a solution like this, your answer is no. Inform him that no matter how many times he asks, you will not change your mind today and that you would rather he not nag to try to persuade you to change your mind. If he nags anyway, do your best to ignore it.

Nagging is a behavior that most of us use to some extent in our lives. I fear it is a practice I used too often with my children. When they would accuse me of nagging, I would tell them I wasn't nagging, just reminding them repeatedly. But when I asked them to help me learn how to stop nagging, they were both willing to offer helpful solutions.

This month, try to eliminate or at least decrease the amount of nagging you do. If you do, your children will appreciate spending time with you more.

● Conclusion

As a parent your job is to help your children succeed. However, this means teaching your children to eventually make their way in the world without you. The more you can teach your children to handle everyday tasks on their own, the more successfully you are doing your job as a parent.

It may feel good to lovingly care for your children by fulfilling their every need, but eventually you will not be there. If they don't learn how to handle their needs without you, you have done them a terrible disservice.

parenting
Q&A

Q *My eleven-year-old daughter, Kerry, doesn't seem to care about her personal hygiene. She doesn't want to take a shower. Every night it turns into a battle. Can you help us solve this problem peacefully?*

A Are you sure that Kerry doesn't want to take a shower? Perhaps she objects to the timing of her shower more than the shower itself. The first step is to ask Kerry if she doesn't ever want to take a shower or if she is unhappy with the timing. Also find out whether her objection to taking a shower is that it indicates that she is moving toward bedtime, something else she may be unhappy about.

Once you have identified where you and she disagree, then your job is to work out how you both can get what you want. This probably means that you are each going to need to compromise some, but both of you may ultimately get more of what you want than is happening now. ▶

parenting

Q&A

If Kerry doesn't mind taking a shower but would prefer to take her shower at a different time—because one of her favorite television shows is on, for example—you and she need to find the time when taking a shower won't interfere with the show (or a game she is playing or whatever activity she is engaged in that is more important to her than showering). If Kerry doesn't want to take a shower because it indicates that it's nearing bedtime, then you and she need to find a bedtime that you both can live with.

However, if Kerry just doesn't like to shower at all, you are facing a different kind of problem. You will need to find out what she doesn't like about showering. Is she frightened of something? Does she feel incompetent in some way? Ask her to describe a quality world picture of being clean by some method other than showering. Or ask her to describe her quality world shower to you. The problem may be as simple as her inability to regulate the water temperature, so she often finds herself in ice-cold or scalding-hot water.

If Kerry tells you that she never wants to ever shower (this is unlikely), explain to her why you want her to shower. Tell her that you will work with her in whatever way she would find most helpful in order to achieve cleanliness.

Finally if Kerry doesn't want to shower, explain what you want, why you want it, and then back off. Eventually she will receive complaints from her social circle. Of course, backing off may be very difficult for you to do, but the harder you push her into showering, the stronger she will resist it. When you place the responsibility on her shoulders, she will be more likely to move toward showering because she isn't faced with having to "lose" to your control.

One last thought about this situation is that you should think carefully and define your specific concerns about Kerry. You state that your daughter "doesn't care about her personal hygiene." And yet, the only problem you describe is showering. Does she wear clean clothes? Does she brush her teeth? Does she wash her hands regularly and at appropriate times? Does she use deodorant (if this is age appropriate and necessary)? Personal hygiene involves much more than showering. By generalizing your definition of the problem, you may be doing a disservice to your daughter and yourself.

7.

Freedom

How much is enough?

M y husband hovers. He won't let our three-year-old daughter do anything because he's so afraid she'll get hurt."

This is not uncommon. Once you look at your vulnerable newborn baby and comprehend the overwhelming task before you, you also begin to see everything in the world as a potential threat that might hurt or harm your little one. As your children get older and bigger, these feelings may begin to diminish. But for some parents this is not so.

● The two mistakes parents make

The father of this small child may be too protective, but on the other end of the protection spectrum are parents of an emerging teenager.

Often these parents back off completely, no longer providing any kind of rules or structures for their children. These parents may believe that it is too late, that their job is over, that their teenager is independent. Sometimes they are also afraid that their children will not listen and won't like them if they impose rules and regulations. It's as though they abdicate their responsibilities as parents. But just because a child is taller doesn't mean that she is prepared or able to handle all of life independently.

Parenting from a position at one of these two extremes is the mistake parents most commonly make. Parents either provide too few options and opportunities for freedom or they back off, allowing complete freedom that causes their child to feel unsafe and unsure.

Imagine you had someone standing at your shoulder all day long cautioning you, telling you not to take your next step, reminding you to watch out for the perils you might face when taking your next breath, and warning you of *Danger! Danger! Danger!* at every turn. Do you think that you would have one of these two reactions? You might feel fearful and worried about all that life has to offer and never feel safe and secure. A second reaction might be that you want to move away from this person who keeps cautioning you and reminding you of all the dangers and perils in the world.

Now imagine that you are a parent imposing this same view of the world on your naïve, impressionable two-year-old. Is it any wonder that these children are often either scared little mice, fearful of leaving their parents' sides, or wild, out-of-control stallions, running far and fast away from their guardians?

Remember, as human beings we are born with the genetic drive for safety and security. If we are constantly reminded that the world is unsafe, we will begin to behave in a variety of ways to gain this sense of safety and security.

● An issue of freedom

In addition to the basic instruction for safety and security, all people, including your children, are born with the need for freedom. Children want to explore all that is in their world, including how they themselves interact with and impact the world. Children's desire to be free hits at the very heart of a parent's greatest fear! You want your children to be safe and secure, to help them survive. Perhaps the greatest challenge for a parent is to honor your child's need for freedom and autonomy in a way that also keeps your child safe.

As a result, freedom is an area where parents frequently make their biggest errors. Parents of young children often hover, monitor, and supervise every move their child makes! Visit a playground and you'll probably see a child happily playing on the monkey bars with a mother a short distance away loudly saying "Be careful!" or "Come down, that's too high! You'll fall and hurt yourself!" or "I told you not to play on the monkey bars!"

These parents are making a double mistake. First, they have given their child more freedom than the *parents* feel comfortable with. And second, these parents are attempting to solve the problem using the external control method of yelling and nagging because they are fearful. Yet the child has his way and plays wherever he likes on the playground while fear makes the parents feel worried about the choice that their child has made. Like it or not, curious children will explore and play on the monkey bars! Although parents are concerned that their child will not be safe on this piece of equipment, yelling or nagging will not help these parents get what they want.

What's the solution? Before going to the playground, discuss with your child what the rules are, what the limits are, and what the boundaries are for playing on all of the fun toys and structures. As soon as you get to the playground, walk to the equipment that is off limits to your daughter, the equipment that your daughter will need you to be with her on to ensure safety, and the equipment she can play freely on while you watch. Then you can stand by, spotting the child on the equipment, just as is done at the Olympics when trained athletes are performing on potentially dangerous equipment. In this way, you're clearly stating the boundaries or limits of liberties you are giving for your child. Remember, freedom does not mean there are no limits; it means creating the limits and allowing your child leeway within these boundaries.

Parents of teenagers often make the opposite mistake. Teenagers are older, more able, and responsible. Teenagers are also more vocal about their demands and unhappiness, so some parents stop setting any limits. When your fourteen-year-old daughter wants to spend time at the home of a new friend whose family you barely know, should you give her a blanket okay? Your fifteen-year-old son has a friend who recently got his driver's license. Together they want to journey to a city some distance away. Do you give your permission? Too often parents tell me that they are afraid to say no because their child will be upset with them or will defy them and secretly do it anyway. What else can they do besides say okay?

What's the solution? The reality is that both children and parents know that teenagers can defy parental wishes and sneak out and do what they want. However, parents have more power and influence than they realize. At this stage, parents need to be clear with their teenagers about what they want and expect. And parents should also be ready and willing to negotiate so that the teenagers are allowed to work with their parents to increase their freedom.

When your fourteen-year-old daughter wants to spend time with a new friend, explain to her that you would like to get to know her friend better too. Perhaps the girls can spend time together at your house first. Or maybe you can be the driver who takes them shopping. Although the girls will very likely want to be on their own at the mall, you can begin to get

parenting tip

I f you're having trouble with a teenager who seems to be always testing your limits, consider this hint from Marilyn, mother of eight-year-old Stacy, eleven-year-old Christine, thirteen-year-old Teddy, and sixteen-year-old Kevin. It may be that your teen needs more freedom, not less.

"Kevin seemed to be testing our limits and pushing boundaries. He ignored any kind of curfew we gave him, neglected his daily chores, and truculently answered our questions when we asked where he was going whenever he left our home. The more he acted like he no longer needed our limits or supervision, the more restrictive and controlling we attempted to be.

"My husband and I started talking. How were we restricting Kevin? Were there some areas of his life that he could and should be managing instead of relying on us to do it for him? Maybe his misbehavior was really a symptom of his not having enough freedom.

"With this idea in mind, the next evening Kevin, my husband, and I discussed ways that we could treat Kevin differently. It was quite an amazing conversation. Kevin did not ask for outrageous liberties. All of his requests seemed surprisingly mature and reasonable. My husband and I did not hesitate to implement the conditions he asked for."

to know this new friend in the car, as you drive them to and from the mall.

When your son wants to be the passenger of a new driver, you need to explain to him what your concerns are. It is understandable that you would be nervous about a new, inexperienced driver negotiating unfamiliar highways. (At least, it is understandable from almost everyone's perspective except your teenager's.) Ask him to limit his trips with new drivers to more familiar territory. Admit to him that you cannot enforce your request. If you acknowledge your lack of power over him, it's more likely he will be responsible with the additional freedom he now realizes that he has.

As difficult and challenging as it is, parents have more power to restrict their children's freedom because they are the authority. Children view their parents as powerful. Spending time reflecting how much freedom you allow or curtail will serve you and your child well. Finding the balance between not being too strict with young children and not abdicating your responsibility with teenagers is not easy, but by working with your children the balance can be found. When parents help their children learn to handle more freedom, parents gain more freedom in their own lives!

● A better alternative

Imagine you are visiting a foreign country. Perhaps the people speak your language—kind of. You can understand the words but not the meaning. You aren't quite sure what the rules and laws are. No one is available to guide, counsel, or help you or you are too proud to ask anyone for help. As you make your way through the day, you are never quite sure of yourself or your next step. You begin to worry that each next step may take you to the edge of the world. Perhaps this step will drop you to your death.

You may handle this strange situation in one of several ways. First, you may be so cautious that you never venture out beyond the safety zone of what you already know, where you already feel safe. In this case you are essentially imprisoned by your fear of the unknown. A second possibility is that with great bravado you boldly and seemingly fearlessly behave with abandon, trying foolish and possibly high-risk activities. In this instance since you don't know what is safe and what is dangerous, you live life with a "what-the-heck" attitude. Everything feels unsafe, so you are not influenced when people accuse you of engaging in high-risk activities—you think it is all high risk anyway. Perhaps your reaction to this situation would be to seek out friends and other older or more experienced folks for the guidance you need. Some of these people may be responsible and lead you down a healthy path. Others may be less than desirable or responsible, but at least they show they care about you by offering some advice.

You probably get the point. When your children become teenagers, they may understand the language, but the meaning seems to have changed for them. Despite their attitude and behavior toward you, their parent, they are still very much in need of your guidance, love, and support. At this point they have many answers of their own and need your answers less often. But they definitely need you available to talk with about the conclusions they are arriving at on their own. Without parents standing by, children may withdraw or engage in high-risk behaviors because all of life feels high risk anyway, or they may turn to other people for the help, support, and guidance they crave.

When your children are teenagers, this is *not* the time to disappear. This is the time to become much more visible. It is also the time to become quieter. Be there, smile, love, praise, get curious, ask questions, and *expect no answers*. The last thing your child wants from you is your opinion, but if he does want your opinion, he will ask for it. Ask for your child's opinion instead. Then listen. If you must offer your opinion to someone, excuse yourself, go to the bathroom, and tell it to the person looking back at you in the mirror.

● How much freedom is enough?

You do not want to provide too much or too little freedom. Both can create difficulties for your child. But how do you know what is too much and what is too little?

Would you describe your child as happy? This question can give you some clues regarding your child and freedom. Here's why. If we made a list of all the behaviors evident in a child who has too little freedom and another list for a child with too much freedom, ironically the lists would be very similar. Generally this list encompasses unruly, irresponsible, disruptive, and disrespectful behaviors. Anyone observing this child would never describe this child as happy. Your first clue regarding your child and freedom can be gathered simply by observing and describing your child. Is your child happy?

If not, then you may suspect that your child does not have the right balance of freedom. The next question you need to ask yourself is what kinds of freedoms, choices, opportunities, and options are you offering your child?

Certainly, the answer to this question will be related to your child's age. You would never say to a two-year-old, "There's the front door, honey. Go out into the world and let me know when you have obtained a good job to support your independence." That is ridiculous. What you do and say with a two-year-old mostly involves organizing her environment to be sure that there is nothing that will hurt her, nor anything that she will inadvertently destroy. Then you keep a careful eye on her most of the time.

But if your four-year-old child respects and listens to you when you say no, answers you and returns to you when you are supervising him on the playground even though he is not close by your side, checks with you before he eats something he found, and has demonstrated that he can play on a piece of playground equipment without you, it is unreasonable and unfair to insist that he not play on it because it makes you nervous. If he wants to try climbing the jungle gym, stand by his side and spot him rather than denying him access because you are afraid he may fall. How will you, and more importantly he, find out his capabilities on the jungle gym if he doesn't even try? The more freedom you give him, the more he will be able to discover which freedoms he can handle.

Just as you would never allow your two-year-old to leave home without you, it is equally ridiculous to say to a sixteen-year-old, "Stay in this playpen." Many parents say that they trust their teenage child but that it is a scary world "out there." They fear for their child when she goes into the world without their constant supervision. How many sixteen-year-olds do you know who are happy and willing to have their parents constantly supervising them?

As has been discussed elsewhere in this book, your job is to say yes to your teenagers as often as possible. But that does not mean you simply say yes to everything without careful discussion and supervision that is available upon demand. The demand may be at the request of your child who has made a poor choice and gotten in over her head, or it may be your demand that your child check in with you, not go to certain places without some sort of adult supervision, and so on.

During those ages between two and sixteen, you make lots of decisions and choices that center on whether you are allowing too much freedom or being too restrictive. Your child can help you see how much is too much or not enough. If your seven-year-old wants you to stay with him when he attends a classmate's birthday party, he is giving you a clue that he doesn't feel safe going to this event without your support and presence. The very next year he may leave the car with barely a backward

Which do you think is the best solution to help both parent and child succeed in getting what they each want and need?

Twelve-year-old Cindy has been caught. All of her life she wanted to go horseback riding. Her parents refused her requests, telling her it was dangerous to ride without lessons, which cost more money than they could afford to pay. Now the parents have discovered that Cindy has been lying to them, sneaking off with her best friend, Lynn, and riding without the benefit of lessons. She has paid for the recreation using her own money. If you were Cindy's parent, what would you do?

● Restrict Cindy for lying and secretly disobeying. Tell her that

glance as you say good-bye. This is helpful information about the level of safety and need for increased freedom your child feels. In only one year his confidence and feeling of competence for how he handles the world without you has increased. His behavior is letting you know.

In addition to observing behavior, you can also discuss with your child her need for your presence or absence. "Do you want me to stick around?" you may ask your daughter. A small smile and nod tells you she cannot spend any time at Lynn's house. In the future the girls will have to spend time together at your home.

- Help Cindy arrange regular riding lessons with a reputable stable and reputable teacher that she pays for herself. As long as Cindy's money lasts, you will provide transportation to and from her lessons.

- Ask Cindy to help you solve this problem with you. Let her know your concern is for her safety. Explain that you understand her desire to have more freedom and to learn this skill. Ask her to work out the solution with you.

These answers go from least freedom provided by the parent to greatest freedom provided by the parent. You may think that the second solution simply rewards Cindy for lying and sneaking around. But the reality is that Cindy can and already has gotten what she wanted without her parents' permission and consent. If her parents are willing to work with her to help her get what she wants, then Cindy will be more willing to work with her parents to help them get what they want, which is for Cindy to be safe.

one thing. "Of course not," tells you something very different.

During those times when you feel you should be present and supervise, listen to and watch your child. Tell your child what you are afraid of. If together you figure out that he has enough responsible behaviors to merit this increased freedom, then you need to determine another way to handle your fear. If your child does not have enough responsible behaviors, then denying your permission is fair.

When your children demonstrate that they have the responsible behaviors to handle additional liberties, your job is to allow them these liberties. As you sit comfortably reading this book, that sounds reasonable and logical. But if you're the parent of a teenager, you know that life is not always so reasonable and logical when you are in the middle of a struggle with your child. Even when you know that your fourteen-year-old daughter has shown good judgment and deals with responsibilities well, you still worry when she wants to walk to the library alone. Your child can take care of herself, but the world is a scary place, with dangers lurking everywhere.

Often what parents do in order to manage the fear they feel for their child is to restrict their child. This may help the parents feel less frightened, but the child feels oppressed and punished for living in a world that frightens his parents. Unfortunately, the result of this struggle is that children sneak out and do what they want without informing their parents.

I know because I was a sneak. I protected my parents from all sorts of information that would frighten them. As a parent, I did not want to put my own children in this position of trying to appear to comply with my wishes while actually enjoying more freedoms than they could handle responsibly.

If a child sneaks out because he thinks his parents will not permit him the additional freedom that he craves and he makes poor choices, whom do you think he will turn to for help? Do you think he is going to ask for help from the parent whose rules he disobeyed? It's not likely.

We should expect that teenagers are going to make poor choices. They are part of the learning experiences that all emerging adults go through. As a parent, I knew that when my child made a poor choice, I wanted him to turn to me or his father to help him brave the consequences of this poor choice. I also knew that if I restricted my child unreasonably, the chances were greater that he would disobey me and do what he wanted, hoping he wouldn't get caught. Then he would really be lost and untethered if he made a bad choice and needed an adult's help. He would dread the negative consequences of turning to me for help.

A powerful and important process can help you during those crucial and hectic times when your child is demanding more freedom and you're not sure what to say. First, your teenagers are not stupid or naïve. They have lived with you long enough to guess what you are going to answer before they even ask for permission to engage in certain activities or go to particular places. Knowing that the odds may be against their receiving a positive answer, many children will calculate when to approach you. They wait for Mom to be cooking while also answering mail, fielding phone calls, and helping their sibling with homework. That's when your teenage daughter will enter the room and casually say, "Anita is having a boy-girl sleepover party at her house on Saturday night and I'm going." Your child is hoping that you are so busy and distracted that you won't quite hear what she says and you will offhandedly okay the event.

Parents of teenagers are also not stupid or naïve. There are times when you aren't quite sure what your child told you. You are indeed distracted and busy. But unfortunately, some parents make the mistake of immediately saying no, no matter what. They think, *If my teenager wants to do it she is probably up to no good, trying to get away with murder. I don't really have time to deal with this right now, but I'm sure she's being devious.* In fact, the teen makes a miscalculation when she hopes that distraction will work to her benefit. When you're stressed and busy, you are less likely to be reasonable and give permission.

But now that you have a better understanding of the developmental process of teenagers, you know that they are driven to seek greater power and freedom. As soon as you tell your teenager no, she is driven to argue with you and to try to get you to change your mind. She is fighting to win at any cost. Even if she didn't particularly want to go to this party, now that you have said no, she is driven to push, argue, and struggle to win the argument and increase her ability to meet her needs for power and freedom.

Here is a much better alternative process that will be invaluable to you: First, when your child asks or tells you what the plan is, and you can't at that moment give the matter your full attention, tell her that you cannot give her an answer yet. Reassure her that you will, just not at this time.

I discourage you from giving "We'll see" as your answer, but that is in part due to a personal memory for me. My mother always said, "We'll see." What that really meant was, "I'm going to give you a negative answer, but I don't want to get into that argument with you now."

Be prepared, however, because when you tell your child that you will give her an answer, just not yet, your child is still going to argue with you. It is very unlikely that your daughter will say to you, "Oh, I understand, Mom. I see that you are very busy doing other things now. I'm happy to wait until you can figure this out and let me know." Despite the fact that your child will probably pressure you, asking you when you will have the answer and insisting that you attend to her request immediately, reassure your child that you will have an answer as soon as you can. Quickly explain that you want to be able to give her request full consideration because it is important to her, and you can't do that now.

At the next quiet opportunity sit with your partner if you are co-parenting or sit with yourself if you are a single parent and discuss or think about the following questions:

1. *Do I have all of the information I need in order to understand what my child is asking permission to do?* If you do not have all of the information necessary, then go back to your child and tell her that you need more information. Tell her exactly what

you need to know and ask her to work with you to get the information. For instance, in the above example, do you know Anita? Do you know Anita's parents? Do you know if Anita's parents plan to be present during this party? Would you like to speak with Anita's parents? If you have all of the necessary information, then go to the next question.

2. *Does my child have the responsible behaviors necessary to handle this amount of freedom?* If your answer is no, then tell your child that the answer to her request is no until she can learn all of the responsible behaviors necessary to handle this additional freedom. Some of these behaviors you may teach her directly and some she may learn through real-life experiences. (Perhaps family camping trips that include boy and girl cousins all sharing a tent may be an example of a life situation that gives her some experience with overnight boy and girl parties.) Again, be prepared. Your child is not going to be happy about an answer that denies her what she wants. But because you have not said "No forever," you have said "No until," she will be willing to accept your answer. Then she will undoubtedly nag you about when you are going to teach her the responsible behaviors she is going to need. If your answer is yes, then go on to the next question.

3. *What am I afraid of?* Be courageous in answering this question. If you are saying no because you are afraid, then your job is to figure out a way to manage your fear other than restricting your child. Your fears are *your* feelings. Don't impose your fears and feelings onto your child if you hope your child will mature into an independent adult. Figure out another strategy for managing your fears rather than limiting your child's activities.

Ask for help to learn how to do this. Often, your partner can be very helpful. Curiously, what you worry about and are afraid of is often not a concern for your partner, and vice versa. Having a partner during these times can be very reassuring, but remember, though being worried and

parenting tip

Mary Beth, mother of two teenagers and one preteen, knows the temptation and perils of engaging in too many unnecessary battles with her children. Here's how she decides when to confront an issue and when to walk away.

"When I am about to get into a discussion or battle or disagreement with one of my children, I ask myself this question: is my child's behavior or request *life altering* or *life threatening*? If the answer is no, then I try and avoid any kind of confrontation.

"Right now my children are in more competitive phases of their growth. They all have greater needs for power and freedom. The potential for arguments and disagreements is limitless. But now I have a specific question to ask myself that helps me decide whether to engage in a battle or avoid it. After all, I may not like the length of Sam's hair or the color of Agatha's hair or the style of Wendy's hair but length, color, and style are not life altering or life threatening. Piercings and tattoos are life altering. Riding in a car with a driver who has been drinking is life threatening."

fearful wasn't part of the bargain you counted on as you became a parent, you have done a good job of handling this fear to this point with or without a partner. As always, your child is giving you another opportunity to learn and grow albeit in areas where you did not want to learn and grow.

● Trust

When your teenage son tells you that he is going to a friend's house to spend Saturday evening, how do you know he is where he tells you he will be? When your daughter wakes up on a school morning complaining of not feeling well, and you know she has a math test she has been worrying about, how do you know she is really sick? When your toddler tells you that he doesn't need to go to the bathroom before you are about to get into the car to run your household errands, can you trust his judgment? As parents, how do you know you can trust your children?

The answer is you don't ever really know. You must make the choice to either trust your children or not. These are not necessarily comforting words. Wouldn't it be a relief to have a litmus test that could give you a definitive trust or don't trust answer to your dilemma?

Obviously, you can take some measures to verify the information your children tell you. For instance, rather than relying on your teenage son's cell phone call, you could call the friend's house and speak to the parents to verify that your child is where he says he is. If you do this, you may feel comforted. But what does that say to your son about your trust in him? You could take your daughter's temperature to see if her illness has affected her body temperature. Perhaps this would confirm to you that your daughter is not making up an illness to avoid a math test. But what would that say to your daughter about your trust in her? You could ask your toddler to visit the bathroom even after he insists that his bladder is empty. But what kind of a message would that send your son about your trust in his ability to monitor his own body functions?

One definition of trust is "the firm reliance on the integrity, the ability, and the character of a person." Can you trust that your children are telling you the truth? Only if you choose to trust them. If you don't, your attempts to monitor and dig for the truth will still leave you wondering whether you can rely on the integrity and character of your children and your choice remains the same—do you trust your child or not? Rather than asking yourself if your child is telling you the truth, a better question is, *Does my child have the ability to competently manage each situation she faces? Can my child rely on her own character?*

As has been discussed before, parents set limits and guidelines to assure their children's safety and success. You have lived longer and you have more experience and more wisdom than your children do. Your rules, expectations, and standards for your children's conduct are based upon this older perspective. However, sooner or later all parents realize that their children will face challenges and choices in the world without their parents being available to consult, guide, and provide the "right" answer. Isn't it better to have a child who can make responsible and safe choices with or without you?

In order to have trustworthy children, you must trust your children. As you trust your children, they begin to trust themselves. Your children begin to rely on their own judgment when they face choices and circumstances that a parent is not there to regulate or monitor. Your children's character, self-confidence, and integrity are built when they choose the responsible path without an adult guiding their every move.

Your children learn the skills to trust themselves and to have faith in their own moral strength when given a chance. When you choose to have confidence in your children, you are choosing to teach them they are trustworthy.

To reinforce your sense of safety and success for your child, teach him the responsible behaviors necessary to handle the situations and circumstances he faces. Then allow your child the freedom and opportunity to practice these behaviors. If your son tells you he is going to a friend's house on Saturday night, tell him that you expect him to be where he says he is. If he is changing locations, you expect to be informed. Let him know that you trust him to keep you informed of his locations. If your daughter tells you she is too sick to go to school, math test or no, trust her. Tell her that you know she has better knowledge of her body's condition from the inside than you do from the outside. If your son tells you he does not need to go to the bathroom before you leave to run errands, believe him. Tell your son that he knows how full or empty his bladder is better than you do.

Choose to trust your child. Tell your child that you trust her. The more often you make this choice and tell your child that you are making this choice, the more experience your child has in trusting herself and feeling trustworthy.

● Conclusion

When you signed on to become a parent, you may not have been aware that you were also signing up for a lifetime of new fears, worries, and concerns. To a certain extent, these fears will be with you forever. You know this is so if your own parents are still alive. Has your mother recently expressed to you her worry and concern about your taking a trip to a place she wasn't sure was safe? As silly as this may have felt at the time, she was expressing to you, her child, the same fear you express to your child. But since we want children to mature into independent, reliable, and responsible adults, we need to give them the opportunities to get there. To do this you must offer and provide more freedom for your child than you may feel comfortable with.

This does not mean simply handing over unlimited freedom and walking away. Slowly increase the amount of freedom as you teach your child the additional responsible behaviors he will need to manage the additional freedom. As your child demonstrates that he can handle ever-increasing amounts of freedom, you will worry less—but you will probably always worry about something. Your concern is simply your genetic drive to feel safe and keep your child safe.

parenting
Q&A

Q *My fourteen-year-old foster son is doing a lot of swearing. He uses this language with his friends as well as online through e-mail. I am not happy about this. Is there anything I can do to get him to stop?*

A For adolescents, swearing seems to be a way to have a greater sense of freedom and power. You have probably already discovered that attempting to externally control his behavior doesn't work. Threatening to ground him, punishing him, or fining him will not succeed. He can and will continue to use foul language if he chooses.

Here are two suggestions that might be useful. First, explain to your foster son your objection to his language. Talk to him about why you feel as you do about it. Further explain that you are well aware that you are unable to make him stop. Admitting to him that you can't control his behavior may help him have a greater sense of power and freedom. Simply explain what your desires are regarding what is acceptable and not acceptable language to you. ▶

parenting
Q&A

Next, at a different time from this first conversation, have an open discussion with your foster son about swearing. Is there ever a time when swearing is inappropriate? Is there ever a time when swearing is appropriate? How do you feel about your own language use? How does he feel about your language use? You might even tell your foster son that you can accept that he swears with his friends but not with teachers or relatives. Is there any liability to using foul language on the Internet?

In other words, engage your foster son in a conversation that doesn't involve moralizing or preaching. After all, he is of an age when he is going to be making increasingly difficult choices regarding his morals and ethics. Why not keep the conversation an open exchange between the two of you? This will have a much greater positive impact on your relationship with each other than any attempts on your part to make him stop. If you ask him his opinion and suggest he self-evaluate, he is more likely to make better choices about his language—eventually.

8.

Bedtime

You're exhausted but they're still up

Bedtime is such a hassle at our home. My nine-year-old son insists that he should stay up later than his eight-year-old sister. But she says she doesn't see why she should have to go to bed earlier than her brother. Every night we go through the same argument, usually ending with me banishing both children to their rooms. It's such a lousy way for all of us to end the day together."

At a recent parenting class, I asked the group how many people experience friction with their children over bedtime. More than half of the group raised their hands. Then I asked how many of them remember being ready and willing as children to go to bed when their own parents asked them to. No one raised a hand.

● Create a plan

As we discussed before, your job as a parent is to slowly increase freedom while simultaneously teaching your children how to handle the additional freedom. Here's the advice I gave the parent with the bedtime problems. Your son seems to be saying that because he is older, he should be afforded greater freedom, so part of his job is to demonstrate his responsibility by working with you to resolve this problem.

Your daughter may feel equally strongly that she has the responsible behaviors to handle the additional freedom of a later bedtime, just like her brother. One way she can demonstrate behaving responsibly means she too will work with you to help solve this problem. Even if

parenting tip

 A seasoned babysitter offers this suggestion for helping a child get to sleep: Put a dab of fragrance on the back of her left hand. Tell her to breathe in the scent deeply. Assure her that by the time the scent has faded she will be asleep.

This works because she is breathing deeply and rhythmically, which helps her become more relaxed and release any worrying or frightening thoughts.

Vary the fragrance. Try ordinary hand cream, a hint of your favorite perfume, even baby powder. Changing the scent will keep her interested enough to want to breathe in the smell.

you believe that only one of your children or neither of them has the responsible behaviors for a later bedtime, you can still work together to solve the problem.

The three of you can make a date for when you are going to sit down together to discuss this problem and work toward its resolution. Try doing this on a Saturday or Sunday in the middle of the day or in the morning—well removed from bedtime.

When the meeting begins, each person has an opportunity to explain what he or she wants. Most likely what you want is for bedtime to be a peaceful time in your home, when all are able and willing to say good night to one another calmly and lovingly. You also want to resolve this problem amicably. You don't want a solution that works only to your advantage. The three of you will come up with a solution together, rather than you alone being expected to create the answer.

After each person has shared his or her picture of how bedtime should go at your home, ask the children, "How can we work this out? What solutions or ideas can we come up with that will allow each of us to get what we want? Perhaps the solutions won't mean that all of us will get everything we want, but perhaps each of us can get some of what we want. Can you think of solutions or a compromise that will move us in the direction of each of us getting what we want while respecting the wants and desires of the others?"

Your goal is to develop a plan that all of you can agree to follow. This may take time and effort. At this point, your job is to patiently guide the children by encouraging them to work it out together. You can add suggestions if they occur to you, but you are not creating answers on your own.

Finally, once the three of you have created a plan, build into your plan a time when you will all evaluate it together. This could be a week later or just a few days later. You want to build opportunities for discussion into the process so that each of you can share with one another how you think the plan is going and if any changes need to be made. This part of the process is as important as creating the original solution.

Your overall goal is to work this out together. The process of the three of you working this problem out together has the greatest chance of moving you all toward peace.

● The drama of nap time

"I am the mother of three children: a daughter age seven years, a son age five years, and a twenty-two-month-old daughter. My problem is with my son. He attends half-day morning kindergarten. Each day after lunch I put the baby down for a nap and ask him to nap as well. Each day brings an argument from him. He wants to know if his older sister is going to have a nap when she gets home from school. When I say no, he becomes furious. Sometimes he works himself into a really big stink, but all the while he is yawning through his tears. How can I approach nap time more peacefully?"

If you have a problem like this mother's, the simplest solution might be changing the name of this time of day. Perhaps your son associates napping with what his baby sister does. He may want to be more grown up, more like his older sister who is not required to nap when she gets home from school. So when you say "nap time," he feels as though you are treating him like a baby.

Calling it "rest time" or "quiet time" might help him. It will establish an environment that allows him to sleep or nap if he needs to, but it doesn't require him to sleep or nap. It simply provides a time during the day when he can recharge his batteries. And that's just the way to describe it to him.

This weekend, why don't you talk with your son about a new plan? Tell him you agree that he is too grown up to take a nap like his baby sister. Explain to him that you and he will each have quiet time or rest time for one hour after lunch. Together, plan where his rest stop will be—perhaps in his bedroom on his bed. But you might want to consider a different, special spot like on Mom and Dad's bed. Ask him to bring with him some quiet toys that he might entertain himself with, like a book or two, some stuffed animals, or a toy car or airplane. Together make a game of it. For the next hour pretend that he is on a special ship

parenting tip

Grandpa Richard explains how he got his six-year-old granddaughter to go to sleep.

"My son and daughter-in-law went out for the evening, leaving me and my wife in charge. The evening went along smoothly. When it was time for the children to go to bed, we got them dressed, tucked them into bed, and read them each a bedtime story. We turned off their lights, kissed them, and bid them good night.

"Not long after this my granddaughter called to us. 'Grandpa, I'm not sleepy. I can't sleep.'

"'That's fine,' I told her. 'You don't have to sleep. When Grandpa is here, you never have to go to sleep.'

"'Really?' she asked.

"'Really,' I told her.

"All became quiet. Fifteen minutes later I went to check on her, and she was fast asleep."

(the bed) and that he must not go off the ship and into the water. As captain, his job is to stay out of the water and on the ship.

If it will help him, he can set an egg timer for one hour. You show him how, place the timer just outside of his room where he can hear the ticking. At the end of the hour, rest time is over. If he has fallen asleep, you may decide you want him to stay asleep. This is something you must decide. Some parents discover that if their children sleep for too long in the afternoon, they have difficulty falling asleep or sleeping through the night.

● Bedtime and homework

Sometimes bedtime issues are really homework issues because the two times are in conflict with each other. Consider this scenario. It's four thirty in the afternoon on a Sunday. Your fifth-grade child comes to you and tells you that she has a big science project that is due tomorrow. Next she admits that she has not even begun the work. What do you do? The choices of doing it for, doing it with, and allowing your child to do the work alone, give you several productive options.

You have unproductive options too, of course. You could also yell at your child, letting her know that she has made a terrible mistake by doing nothing until the last minute and then coming to you, hoping you will save the day. Although this may be how you feel, venting your frustration and concerns onto your daughter at this time will do nothing to resolve the issue. It won't even give you relief. Instead of feeling better, you'll probably end up feeling guilty when you see how much worse your daughter feels after the lambasting. If your daughter must also deal with her own upset emotions, she will not be able to work efficiently. Even though you may hope that this "good talking to" will help her learn a lesson about planning ahead, for the most part it will teach her a lesson about how you handle upsets.

So which of these productive options would you choose?

Plan A: Suggest to your daughter that she plan for tomorrow. Give her the option of role playing with you what she is going to say to her teacher. Warning—if you choose this plan, be prepared to negotiate with a child who may not sleep well and may wake up with a mysterious ailment.

Plan B: Ask your daughter to gather her schoolbooks and meet you at the computer. Together, work diligently until just before her bedtime, accomplishing as much as you are able to. You may want to suggest to your daughter that you role play what she will say to her teacher the following day if the work does not get finished.

Plan C: Ask your daughter to gather her schoolbooks and meet you at the computer. Together, work diligently until her bedtime. When she goes to bed, you stay up all night and successfully complete another fifth-grade science project.

● Conclusion

Whether your concern is your own sleep requirements or your child's, from the moment your child is born, sleep is an issue. The need for adequate rest and sleep is one of the biological genetic drives all people are born with. Creating the process to establish the balance between what you want and what your child wants and working together to find the solution will serve you well in other areas too, so take the time and work this out to everyone's satisfaction. Not only will everyone be well rested, but also together you will have learned to respectfully work out how you can all get some of what you want.

Which of the described options do you think teaches your child the most? Which gives her more freedom while simultaneously teaching her how to handle the additional freedom responsibly? Which do you think would help her learn how to work differently the next time she has a school project? Which of these choices will help your daughter successfully meet her need for power? Which of these choices will help you feel like a competent and loving parent? Which will help you move in the direction of meeting your need to help your child become independent?

parenting

Q&A

Q My thirteen-year-old son, Jack, declared that he no longer needs a bedtime imposed by me and his mother. Although I agreed, I am now worried because he is staying up until one in the morning and later. Any suggestions?

A Good for you for slowly increasing Jack's freedom as you help him develop the responsibility to handle the additional freedom. What you are experiencing are the growing pains that we parents feel as our children practice coping with their new autonomy. At the beginning, learners are not very good at practicing any new skill. Remember when Jack was just learning to walk? He didn't immediately stand and step out without any difficulty. He stood, found his balance, took a step, and fell. He then probably stood again, found his balance again, stepped out, and took two or three steps before he fell again. On and on this practice went until he was finally able to stand and walk without any problem. ▶

parenting

Q&A

As he is learning this next step toward independence and responsibility, Jack will continue to stand (declaring he no longer needs a bedtime imposed by you), take a step (staying up later than is perhaps good for him), and fall (staying up until one o'clock and waking up the next day very tired). It will help you to cope now if you recall the experience of when Jack was learning to walk. When he fell you didn't immediately pick him up and carry him, did you? If you did, he never would have learned to walk on his own.

You are probably also worrying about his performance in school as well as how extracurricular activities will be affected if he has not had enough rest. But if you jump in too soon to try to influence the choices that Jack is making on his own about his bedtime, it will be similar to picking him up every time he fell when he was learning to walk. In fact, it might be even worse. You run the risk of undermining Jack's confidence in his ability to make good decisions for himself.

Instead, use another key technique of the peaceful parenting process. Ask Jack to self-evaluate. How well does he think he is doing at making his own decision about bedtime? Does he notice any positive consequences from this change? Does he notice any negative consequences? Is he having any trouble or challenges that you can help him with? If you can remain neutral, without imposing or even implying your judgments, you may also point out to Jack the results you have observed (not the ones you fear may happen) about Jack's choice of a bedtime.

As long as you are willing to keep an open dialogue going with Jack, sharing with him your own experiences choosing your own bedtime (if he is interested), he will be more willing to discuss with you this new capability he is learning. If he believes that you will take back this freedom if he doesn't answer the question correctly, then he will be less likely to have an honest discussion with you.

As with any new freedom, the initial extremes of his behavior will temper with time. He is probably staying up late now because he can, but once the thrill of staying up late is coupled with his experiences of the consequences of this choice, Jack will begin to make more realistic and healthy bedtime choices.

Siblings

Foes and co-conspirators

magine that you and your family are several hours into a long car trip. So far the children in the backseat have been relatively quiet and cooperative. Then, without notice or explanation, one child starts complaining about the other.

BROTHER: Stop looking at me.
SISTER: I'm not looking at you. You're looking at me.
BROTHER: No, I'm not.

The car is silent for a moment.

BROTHER: Knock it off!
SISTER: I'm not doing anything! You're a jerk.
BROTHER: No, *you're* a jerk.

● Why can't they get along?

Perhaps the greatest daily test of this peaceful parenting process is sibling rivalry, sibling disagreements, and sibling bickering. Your children's arguments may seem relentless. Is there no limit to what can spark angry words? Is it really so important who sits where, who does which chore, or who started the battle in the first place? Can a parent be expected to keep track of whose turn it is to go first, who gets the extra helping of pizza or the extra chore, or who can stay up the latest? If you had nothing else to do during the day other than monitor your children's relationship with each other, you still couldn't stop the flow of tedious, unpleasant interactions between your children.

Some parents worry that their children's relationship will forever be acrimonious.

"How do I help my children get along better? One minute they seem to love each other, the next I fear they will kill each other."

"The bickering and battling between my children is driving me to the brink. Is there any way to help these children stop fighting?"

These are just a few of the many questions that parents ask about sibling rivalry. Perhaps the idea of using a peaceful strategy as a parent sounds great, but what kind of initiative for peace and love between brothers and sisters can you implement?

● Annoying your sister can be fun!

Remember that one of the genetic instructions that children are born with is the urge for fun. Bullying a younger brother or sister can be fun. However, it is not fun for parents. It may not even be fun for the sister or brother who is being picked on. But it can be a form of entertainment and relief from boredom.

Consider that long car ride. The children bicker back and forth until one escalates the battle by screaming, hitting, or calling the parents into the mix. From the children's point of view the long, dull car trip has been altered with the mild entertainment of a back seat battle.

Here is another typical exchange. Your children are together in the family room. From a nearby room you can hear most of what is occurring. As far as you can tell, quiet and calm prevail. But the next moment your younger daughter is wailing, crying, and complaining that her older sister hurt her, hit her, or in some other way was being unfair to her. As you enter the room, your eldest daughter looks guiltily at you. Your younger daughter runs to you for protection and comfort.

Here is what you didn't see: The younger sister was bored. The television program the two sisters were watching was dull. They had gone too long without fun, so the younger girl reached over to tickle her older sister's feet. The elder girl drew her feet back. After waiting for her sister to get involved in the game, the younger sister leaned over to try and tickle her sister's feet again, getting a little more aggressive this time. Again, the elder girl simply withdrew her feet, from her sister's reach. Finally, the younger sister couldn't wait for more action so she grabbed her older sister's ankles, yanked until she had pulled out her feet and did her best to tickle her sister into a tickle wrestling match. The older sister was not interested in this game. She pushed her younger sister away and, in the process, knocked her off the couch.

Baby Sister was really unhappy then. Not only was she unable to get her sister to play a better game than simply watching a dull television show, now she had been humiliated by being knocked to the ground. So when she cries for her mother's help, she is crying from sorrow and, more importantly, for revenge. If her big sister won't play with her, then she deserves to get into trouble, to be punished by their mother.

If you have brothers and sisters, do you remember the hours of fun and entertainment provided by your built-in playmates? For just a moment suspend your vision of family life from the parental point of view, and realize that brothers and sisters bickering and arguing is often a source of fun and entertainment for the children. This doesn't mean you need to like it or tolerate it. For now, just acknowledge it.

Some parents grew up in families without siblings and don't have any frame of reference for how siblings behave. Perhaps they had always imagined an ideal scenario in which the imagined brother or sister played the role of the always-available, ever-amiable best friend. For those of us who did have siblings, it seems that somehow when we become parents, we completely lose all memory of what life was like

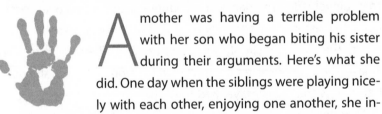

parenting tip

A mother was having a terrible problem with her son who began biting his sister during their arguments. Here's what she did. One day when the siblings were playing nicely with each other, enjoying one another, she interrupted them. She asked them why they were able to get along so well together during this game and also how they might handle an argument differently from their usual way. Neither of them had an alternative idea, so she suggested one.

She presented them with a "magic ball," a simple multicolored rubber ball she had purchased. She told them that as soon as either one of them felt a conflict brewing, he or she should pick up the ball. This would be a signal for the other to back off. It also meant that the two of them needed to come to her so she when we were children with our own brothers and sisters.

If you were the smaller, younger child, you knew just what to do to provoke your older sibling into "hurting" you. Then you would cry much louder than was necessary and wait. Eventually, one of your parents would intervene and voilà—you had maneuvered and manipulated your brother into getting into trouble.

If you were the older, larger sibling, you knew that your younger pest of a brother or sister would push you to the edge. You knew that with one large swat you could get this baby to leave you alone. And so you would push, shove, punch, or pinch this annoying child. The next

could help them solve their conflict.

In the beginning she had to enter into arguments that had already started and hand one of them the ball. Then she would ask the magical question, "Stephanie, what is it that you want that you are trying to get by using bullying words with Kenny?" Or, "Kenny, what is it that you want that you are trying to get by biting Stephanie?" Once she found out what the child wanted, she would help him or her learn another way to get it.

She was patient. At first, it seemed as though she was the only one who was picking up the magic ball. But after about two weeks, the children started using the ball. And now an even more wonderful result has happened. The children have learned the magic question so well that when one picks up the ball, the other asks what she or he wants without the mother having to intervene at all.

thing that would happen is your brother would cry as if you had really injured him. Then your father or mother would come to the baby's rescue, admonishing you that you are older and should know better. It was infuriating! No matter how much you protested that you had been set up by your brother, your parents just didn't want to hear your side of the story.

Older siblings are not simply innocent victims of their younger brother or sister, however. The elder sibling can trick his baby sister into thinking salt is sugar, or younger brother into pulling the cat's tail to get it to sing or some other mischievous prank that may lead to the younger sibling getting into trouble with their parents. Older siblings delight in being able to manipulate their younger sibling for their own personal entertainment.

● The balance of power

Even if the conflicts your children engage in begin as a way to satisfy their need for fun, they quite often result in a power struggle. Between children and parents there exists a real and perceived power differential. Both parents and children believe that parents, as the adults, are more powerful than the children in the family. When brothers and sisters argue and battle with one another, it is generally a battle between equals. When a parent intervenes, the child who wins the parent's approval or sympathy has gained more power. Parents have now taught their children an effective strategy for meeting their need for power. Children will use this strategy over and over again. Having given their validation, parents have set their children up to be in a perpetual battle for parental approval and parental power.

The unconscious thought process becomes *If I can get into an argument with my brother and get my father on my side, then I win the*

parenting tip

 Naomi, mother of five-year-old frater-
nal twins, Zachary and Samuel, found
the solution to some of the bickering between the two boys was a little less
togetherness.

Rather than insist that the boys share all their toys, she has
designated some as Zach's toys and others as Sam's toys. They
still have some toys that they share, but each has a greater
sense of ownership and power over his own toys.

Also, rather than insist that they work together to accomplish their household chores, she has given each child his own
chore to complete himself. Sam's job is to set the table; Zach's
job is to feed the dog. Each boy knows he has his own job.

The overall result of all of these changes is that each boy
now feels as though he has more power and freedom. There is
less arguing and bickering between the boys.

argument and, more importantly, get more power than my brother. Is this
the kind of behavior and strategy you want your children to learn? If
you persist in taking sides, declaring one child to be more responsible
or more to blame for an argument, you have set your family up for long,
long years of children battling, tattling, and provoking each other into
power struggles.

● A better way

Here's what you can do instead. Your job is to teach your children how to work out their differences. But first you need to decide if every incident needs or warrants your intervention.

We'll start with some theory. Remember, children are born with the genetic instructions for safety, love, power, fun, and freedom. Children behave in the world in ways that they hope will satisfy one or more of these urges. Because siblings spend so much time with each other, they attempt to meet their needs with each other, often using competitive behaviors.

Luckily, children can also satisfy their cooperative needs for love and fun with each other. Thus you will see brothers and sisters playing wonderful, magical, imaginary games together.

As a mother of identical twins, I am gratefully aware of the beauty of the relative cooperation and conviviality that has always been a part of my sons' relationship with each other. They bickered over whose turn it was to empty the dishwasher until we came up with a system for assigning each boy a specific dishwasher shelf to unload. They argued over playing with the same toy at the same time, as well as who would sit "shotgun" in the car. But harmony between the boys was more the rule than any kind of rivalry, arguing, or bickering. Each boy believed that if his brother had accomplished something he hadn't, it was only a matter of time before he would too. So when David hit a home run out of the ballpark in Little League, Paul knew that he too would eventually do the same. Because they were twins, each was in the unusual position of regarding his brother's accomplishments as something within his own abilities.

Early in the boy's lives I remember making a clear resolve not to become the judge or arbiter of their arguments. *If I decide who is right and who is wrong now, I'll be doing that for the rest of my life,* I thought to myself. That was not a job I wanted.

peaceful parenting quiz

Which of the following do you think will help siblings behave less like foes and more like co-conspirators?

● Ask your children to race against each other to put on pajamas, brush their teeth, and get into bed.

● Ask your children to team up and race against you to clean up toys in the playroom. They will put away all red toys. You will put away all toys with wheels.

● Ask your children to see if they can sing louder than you and your wife while you all clean the kitchen together.

● Have your children race to see which of them can complete her household chore first.

My hope is that you now see that when you ask your children to become a team and race against their parents, it is more likely that they will act as co-conspirators. When you ask them to race against each other, they are more likely to act as foes.

I knew that if I reprimanded one of the boys for something, I would be upsetting the precarious balance of power they were establishing with each other.

As the parent, I was perceived as having more power. If I became *the* judge, the boys would spend much of their time arguing with each other to try to win my approval or my agreement, thus gaining additional power.

Children are very quick to learn that provoking and tattling is an effective way to gain power over their sibling. As parents, do you want children to learn to get along and perhaps like each other enough to eventually become friends?

I decided my job was to help the boys learn to resolve their arguments and disagreements between themselves. This included establishing rules of fair play such as these that all could abide by.

● If one person wants the radio on in the car and the other person wants the radio off, the person who wants silence wins. You can create music in your head in silence, but it is very difficult to create silence when the radio is playing.

● When I ask for help and one boy volunteers his brother, it is he who will be the volunteer.

● A sign is posted for whose turn it is to empty the garbage. After the job is completed it is that boy's job to turn the sign over so that his brother's name appears as the next one to complete the chore. If he forgets to turn the sign, the next time the garbage needs emptying his name will appear, and it will be his turn again.

There is nothing wonderful or special about these rules and guidelines. The idea is that together we worked out some ways to handle some specific situations that continually led to bickering and arguing. Rather than listening to their bickering or trying to resolve each battle for them, we created general "rules of the game"—the game being getting along with each other in our home.

● What can you do?

Are you expecting that your children will be in peaceful, quiet harmony with each other? One parent who grew up as an only child told me that he wanted to have lots of children because his children would always have someone to play with. What he wasn't prepared for was that his children would also have someone to battle with. In fact, he worried that he and his wife were doing something wrong because their sons argued, bickered, and wrestled with each other.

Do you also see your children's upsets and disagreements as a symptom of something being wrong? Is it possible that your children provoke each other for the sake of fun and entertainment? This may not always be the case, but probably it happens more frequently than you realize.

How do you handle your children's arguing and bickering using this peaceful parenting process? First, realize that children are going to disagree and be contentious with one another. It is part of how they are learning to get along with each other and with other people in the world outside of the family.

Second, decide that your most important job is to help your children learn how to work through conflict and get along even when they disagree. This includes working *with* your children to establish rules or guidelines for how you all agree to handle a specific situation, especially when you hear the same argument over and over again.

Finally, if the arguments are more than you can stand, separate. This might mean you leave and go to another part of the house so you don't have to listen to the bickering that is disturbing you. It also might mean you ask the children to separate from one another in whatever way works best. That may be sending one to her room for a while or sending one to the living room and the other to the dining room.

Obviously, you can take a hands-off approach only when the fight is verbal. If the children begin hitting or being physical with one another, you should separate them immediately. Your job is not to settle the argument, but it is to be sure they are both physically safe from one another.

If they frequently argue in the car or someplace you cannot separate them, talk about how you will all handle this ahead of time. This agreement might include changing the subject, removing the object they are fighting over, or asking them to pretend their sibling is invisible so whatever that sibling says or does can't disturb the other child. But if an argument still arises, simply remind your children of your agreement on dealing with arguments.

Be sure you pay attention to times when your children are getting along and enjoying one another. Take note of the fun, good times whenever they are part of your family life. Remember, your brain pays attention when life is different from what you want, when something seems wrong. You have to go out of your way to notice when events and people's behavior are as you think they should be. When your children are friends, enjoying one another's company and companionship, it doesn't register in your brain and you don't automatically pay attention. Make sure you begin to be conscious of those moments.

There may be more fun and cooperation between your children than you realized. The arguing and bickering may grab your unsolicited attention but by being conscious of the great range of your children's interactions with each other you will give yourself more opportunity to celebrate the loving that is part of your children's relationship.

● Conclusion

Children who are lucky enough to have siblings learn early about the art of developing relationships. Having other children in the family

helps children learn how to get along with other people and how to resolve differences. Initially, this resolution process may take the form of
an argument or a battle. Your job, as the parent, is to teach your children
how to resolve differences between or among themselves without resorting to violent words or actions. As odious or annoying as these
conflicts are to your immediate sense of peace and harmony, they rep-
resent your opportunity to begin teaching your children important,
lifelong skills. You are teaching them to develop healthy relationships
with other people outside of the family. Learning to be friends and to
respectfully resolve differences are talents that last a lifetime.

parenting

Q&A

Q *My boys, who are ages seven and nine, have me stumped. When I ask Darren what he wants to get by hitting his brother he replies, "To hurt him back the way he hurt me!" This isn't the response I was expecting. He says it every time I ask the magical question. What I find I'm doing next is venturing off into a lecture about how he should treat his brother well, that his brother and he are the best friends that they will ever have, and so on. I see in my son's eyes that he tunes me out. Help!*

A Children are incredibly creative and unpredictable people. You ask your son one thing, hoping you know what his answer will be, and then he surprises you by taking the conversation in a totally unexpected direction. Although you are frustrated, try to remember to stop and be thankful that your son is an individual, with a unique vision of the world.

The answer to your question is relatively easy. You ask Darren, "What do you want that you are trying to get by hitting your brother?" He answers, "To hurt him the way that he hurt me." Next, follow your question with, "And what do you hope you will get when you hurt your brother back?"

Remember that all behavior is purposeful. Darren tells you his purpose for hurting his brother is retaliation. There is still an answer that lies hidden behind this response. Perhaps Darren hopes if he hurts his brother back that his brother will never hurt him again. Maybe Darren wants to prove to his brother he can't be pushed around. Maybe Darren simply hopes that his brother will give up and give in if Darren hurts him badly enough.

There is something that Darren wants that he is hoping he will get by hurting his brother back. You need to continue asking your questions until you find out what it is that Darren wants that he is hoping he will get by hurting his brother back. Hang in there and keep asking.

In the meantime, you can also ask Darren's brother the same question. What does he want that he is trying to get by hurting Darren? It could be that he wants to annoy and pester his brother. It could be that he wants command of the remote control, the television, the compact disc player, or the favorite chair in the family room.

It sounds as though the boys get into their battles for one reason, but then the battle continues for another. See if you can help the boys trace this back to the original intention behind the first strike.

It's a wonderful idea to talk with the boys about their friendship—the one that exists today and the one that may exist in the future. Save this conversation for another time, however, when the three of you are enjoying each other's company. Perhaps at bedtime you could talk with each boy or both boys together about fun fun they had with each other that day. If appropriate, you ▶

parenting

Q&A

might also talk with your sons about the friendship you have with your siblings. If you spend time with your extended family, they also get to see firsthand the friendship you have with your siblings.

Don't give up. You're on the right track.

10.

Teenagers

A parent's biggest nightmare?

Today, cell phones and iPods have changed the dynamics of car trips. Recently I was stopped at a red light and in the lane next to me was a father and his preteen daughter. Even though this father and daughter were in the car together, they were in very different places. The father was talking on his cell phone, and his preteen daughter was singing along to her iPod. Of course I did not have enough information from that brief observation to make any sort of fair evaluation of what was happening. I did think to myself that this father was missing a golden opportunity to connect with his daughter. They were together in one of the best connecting places, the family car.

● Be ready: children grow up fast

Our children will become teenagers well before we are ready for that stage. It seems to be a strange and mysterious paradox about parents and children that as their children become older and more ready for the changes and challenges that they face in their lives, parents become less ready to accept their children's growing desire for independence.

I have heard many parents express this reluctance as worry about how their children will cope with their next challenge. For example, they may say, "How can my child be attending middle school this September? He is still so young. Will he be victimized by the older children? Will he be up to the increasingly difficult schoolwork? Will he be able to keep track of his more complicated school schedule that includes changing classrooms?"

These may be a few of the concerns that you have as a parent. But then once you watch your child attend middle school for a week, you discover that not only is she surviving, she is actually flourishing. She was ready. You weren't.

Some patterns can be established sooner rather than later, before your child is in the preadolescent or adolescent stage, that will help you both when your child arrives at that stage. Here is one idea.

During your child's teenage years, your desire to talk with your child will increase. After all, this person is becoming more articulate and more opinionated. The level of discussion can be more mature and sophisticated. Ironically, your child wants to talk with you less right at the time that you are more interested in talking. One of the best places to talk with your child, an area where your child will be more willing and interested in conversation, is the car. As you drive your child from one place to another, you have a wonderful, unforced opportunity to talk. Your child can't escape. But if you don't learn how to avoid some distractions now, well before your child is a teenager, you may lose the one place where talking together can happen naturally. This chapter has some tips that will help you prepare for future conversations with your teens.

● Communicating with your teen

As Shauna became a teenager, her mother was concerned about the selfishness of her behavior, her unkind words and deeds toward her sister, and her apparent disrespect of her parents. Rather than the usual threats of grounding her or demands for better behavior, I suggested that Shauna's mother talk with Shauna during their "nice feeling" times together. She told me they didn't have those times anymore. This could be at the core of their problems. I suggested that she spend time with Shauna, but not to talk about their upsets. Instead, they needed to find something that they could enjoy together.

The mom was very skeptical about this advice because she was afraid she would give Shauna the impression that all that Shauna had been doing lately was okay. But Shauna's mom also missed the loving relationship she had had with Shauna. So despite her concerns, she followed my suggestion.

At first their time together was stiff. Shauna seemed worried that her mom was setting a trap for her. But every week they made plans to spend at least one afternoon with each other. Sometimes they went shopping. Other times they went out to lunch or took a walk in a local park. They didn't have any specific agenda other than spending time with one another.

The results have been wonderful, Shauna's mother reports. She feels as though she knows her daughter better now than she has in years. Shauna knows her mother better too. Shauna's initial resistance has melted and now her enthusiasm for their time and for their relationship matches her mother's own enjoyment.

And as predicted, the meanness and selfishness have decreased considerably. Shauna is not a perfect, obedient child. But she is nicer to everyone in the family and is more willing to pitch in and help around the house. Recently her mom overheard Shauna and her sister laughing together.

● How to talk with your teen

The job all parents try to do successfully is to slowly increase the amount of freedom they offer their children as they teach the responsible behaviors to handle this additional freedom. The following is an example of a conversation between a parent and teenage son that shows respect for each other's needs.

> "Mom, I won't be home right after school today. I'm going with some guys to the mall to look at the new iPhones."

> "Who are you going with? How are you getting there? Are you coming directly home after that? How will you get home?" asks the mother.

Note that this mother is checking to see how her child is planning on handling this additional freedom. But despite the fact that her child has declared his intentions, this mother is acting as though he is asking permission rather than accepting his decision outright.

You've no doubt heard it from more than one source: Choose your battles. Rather than getting into a power struggle and focusing on the fact that her child is now telling her what he is going to do rather than

parenting tip

The radio in the car is often a source of conflict—someone wants it on; someone else wants it off. Try this rule: The person who wants the radio off wins. This worked well with my boys from the time they were little. If both children and I wanted the radio on, we would listen to music on our trip. But if only one of us wanted silence, then no music was played.

This rule's bonus payoff came when the boys became teenagers. Not only did they want the radio playing, they wanted it blaring. How could I possibly take advantage of those precious moments to talk with them if the radio was blasting? It suddenly became easy. All I had to do was state that I desired silence! And in the silence, we talked.

asking permission, she pretends to herself that he is asking. If you can develop this ability to pretend it will save you aggravation and your child will feel more powerful.

"I'm going to Jason's house. His mother has agreed to give us all a ride. In fact, she said she is going to do some of her own shopping there. Then she'll give me a ride home."

With those questions answered, this mother continues, "Are you planning on buying a phone today?"

"No. I think they cost too much money, and I don't think that many new features have been added. But Jason doesn't have a phone at all so I wanted to go with him and check it out. He asked me to go to give him advice."

This all seems reasonable. This mother knows how proud her son feels being the consultant about gadgets among his friends. This gives him a great sense of power. Plus, she also knows that he has shown good judgment in the past, forgoing buying a new electronic device just because it is the latest. He is more cautious about holding onto his money.

"Sounds like a good plan. Do you need me to write you a note to get off the bus at Jason's bus stop?"

"Nah. Jason's mom is picking us up right from school."

"Okay. Be sure you call me if you change plans. Otherwise, what time can I expect you?"

"I know I'll be home by six o'clock at the latest. I have homework I'll need to do, and I want to watch that television show tonight. And yes, before you even ask, if I'm going to be more than thirty minutes later than our agreed upon time, I'll call you."

This is an ideal conversation between parent and teenage son. The son wants more freedom. His mother is happy to agree to this because her son is demonstrating the responsible behaviors necessary to handle the additional scope of activity and autonomy. Although the dialogue that is offered in full sounds complete, the rest of the story is in all the years that this mother and child worked together leading up to this.

Open communication begins early when both parents and children keep each other informed of their plans and schedules. When parents deny children their permission for a specific request, parents have another opportunity to continue their good communications. Parents should explain their reasoning for their denial and then plan how they can work together to help their children learn what is necessary to gain their permission. When parents honor their children's desire for privacy as well as ask for and attempt to share thoughts, goals, highlights, and challenges, they are fostering good and open communication with their teens. Most importantly, parents of adolescents need to spend most of their time listening and not lecturing. Parents who practice this important tip will have teenage children more likely to continue communicating with them.

● Sex

Here's another conversation between a parent and teen.

"It's just not fair," says sixteen-year-old foster daughter Maureen to her foster mom. "You always say no to everything I want to do. I don't think you really care about me or love me. If you did, you would let me do the things I want!"

"I know this is hard to believe, Maureen, but the fact that I don't let you do everything you want to do really shows how much I do care about you," replies her foster mom.

"You just don't trust me. You're worried about me getting involved with boys and sex. You don't want me to have any fun," says Maureen.

"That's not true. But I also think I have a problem. Do you know

parenting tip

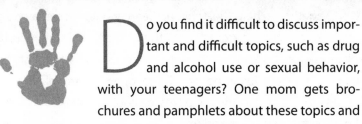

Do you find it difficult to discuss important and difficult topics, such as drug and alcohol use or sexual behavior, with your teenagers? One mom gets brochures and pamphlets about these topics and leaves them in the bathroom, strategically placed. The pamphlets do not replace her attempts at conversations, though they do disappear from the bathroom. She has actually found several in her daughter's room and in her son's backpack.

This is a good way to be sure that your children have access to important information that is potentially embarrassing to you or them. Your local library, health center, or school nurse probably has many of these public-service pamphlets available. You can also download them online.

why I don't want you doing everything that you want to do? It's not because I don't want you to have fun. And yes, I am worried about you and boys and sex. But do you know what my problem is?" asks her foster mom.

By now Mom has Maureen's attention.

"I'm frightened. I'm worried that the kinds of activities that you want to do that you consider fun will hurt you. I'm scared that you will find yourself in a situation that you can't handle. I'm worried about your safety. That's my problem.

"I also realize that I'm not being fair in holding you back because I'm scared. I need your help. I want to figure out a way that we can work together. I want to start saying yes more often to your requests. If I have more information about what you're doing, if I have more reassurance about how you would handle problems or difficulties that you may face, then I'll feel less afraid. Even though I still might be scared, my job is to figure out how to handle my fears. I've resolved not to hold you back from learning and experiencing your life just so I can feel less frightened. Are you willing to work out plans with me so I can say yes to you more often?"

Can you imagine yourself having a conversation like this with your teenager?

We are born with the biological urge to behave sexually. The survival of our species depends on this very strong biological urge. Without it, there would be no more children, no more human beings. No matter how much parents may want to, they cannot keep their children from being driven sexually.

Just as is true with all the other genetic drives we are born with, our children need our guidance and help in learning how to satisfy this urge responsibly. Hoping you can teach them to abstain is not enough. Do you think you can teach your children to abstain from breathing? At a certain age, because of biology and strong hormones, children are driven to engage in sexual behavior. Our job is to teach our children how to handle these urges responsibly and safely.

The most recent research indicates that the program advocating teenage sexual abstinence is delaying young people's first experience of having sex (traditional vaginal intercourse) by about eighteen months. However, these adolescents are still engaging in other kinds of sexual activity. And because these same programs are teaching that condoms are ineffective, adolescents are engaging in unprotected

Which do you think creates an atmosphere where your teen is more likely to talk with you?

● Preview a controversial R-rated movie, and then watch it at home with your teen. Ask his opinions about certain controversial issues. Ask him if he is interested in your opinions too.

● Find articles from the newspaper or an online news source about teens who drink and drive. Give these articles to your teen to read, explaining why you are concerned about her safety.

● Ask your teen which of his friends' parents he respects the most and why. Which of his friends' parents does he not respect and why?

● Ask to see and review your teen's completed homework assignments.

Whenever you ask open-ended questions without supplying the answer, you are more likely to create an atmosphere for conversation with your teen, where each of you speaks and listens. Be warned, however, this still does not guarantee that your child will talk with you. This just increases the chances that she will.

sexual activity, putting themselves at greater risk. Youths who are sexually active, in the traditional sense, are also less likely to use condoms. Our children are at greater risk than ever when it comes to engaging in unprotected sex.

● Conclusion

A continual tension between our desire to keep our child safe and our child's desire to be free is an integral component of the relationship between child and parent. This tension begins when children are born. From the minute children leave the womb, parents worry about their safety. From the minute they leave the womb, children are moving away from us toward their own freedom and independence.

Your job is to learn how to manage your own fears, not to impede your child's growth and development so you can feel safer. Teaching your child to manage being in the world safely and responsibly may help you feel less fearful. Along the way you may also discover how to more effectively meet your own needs and follow your own genetic instructions. All of this must be done in an atmosphere of love and respect between you and your child.

parenting

Q&A

Q *My family and I have recently moved from a smaller, more rural town to a lovely big house in the city. My oldest daughter, Brooke, age fourteen, has made new friends and seems happy, but I'm not. Her behavior has become more defiant and disrespectful. Plus, she is dressing in a manner that I'm not pleased about. She looks too grown- up, too sexual. Do you have any ideas or suggestions that might help?*

A Keep in mind two things: First, your daughter is following her basic need for love and belonging. With teenagers, this means she is driven to make friends with her new peers. Part of what she is doing to make these connections is to be more like the people she is trying to connect with. This includes dressing like others, talking like others, and initiating interests in new areas that others are interested in.

Second, your daughter is fourteen years old. If you were still living in your former home, she would probably be changing there as well. She is experimenting with who she is and who she wants to be. Perhaps her style change is more dramatic in the city than it would have been had you not moved from the country, but this change would have happened anyway. Ask some of your friends who are still living in the country if they have noticed any differences with their adolescents. Some of their complaints will probably sound familiar to you.

Just because you now understand more about what is happening with your daughter doesn't mean that you can't do anything, however. But take care that in your attempts to share your concerns with your daughter, you do not do anything to try to force her to change. If you do, you will probably fail at changing her. All that you will accomplish will be to weaken your connection.

Approach your daughter during a relaxed, happy moment to initiate the conversation. Tell her that you have noticed how she is changing. Try to share this observation with her in a neutral way. She may still hear it as negative and judgmental, but do your best to explain to her that you are not trying to criticize and judge but that your goal is to understand her better and be connected to her.

Ask her why she is wearing the type of clothing she is wearing. What does she like about it? Do other friends of hers wear similar styles? Explain to her that if she can talk with you about these changes you will be more able to accept some of her choices even though you may not like them. You may need to have this conversation more than once, but be careful not to have this conversation so frequently that she begins to feel nagged about it. You might also mention some of the changes that you have made in your attempts to fit in to the city crowd better.

During a time when you feel connected with your daughter, ▶

parenting

Q&A

talk with her about how she talks to you. Explain to her what you mean when you say she is being disrespectful and defiant. Let her know that you feel hurt (which you probably do underneath your anger) and disconnected when she treats you this way. Ask her if she can talk with you respectfully even when she disagrees with you. If you treat her with respect even at times of disagreement, then it is more likely that she can learn to do the same.

Finally, if you are worried about your daughter's blossoming sexuality, talk with her about sex. Share with her your opinion and then listen, with your goal being to completely understand her thoughts, concerns, and opinions. As adults we may see the styles teenage girls are wearing and judge them as too sexual, but many teenage girls see what they wear as fashionable, not sexual.

Do your best to support and love your daughter as she matures. Try not to blame her new behaviors on your geographic changes, but instead accept them as the next step in the joy of parenting. The fact that your daughter has been successful in making new friends and being happy throughout this geographic change at a time when her body, mind, and spirit are maturing is something for you to be proud of.

11.

Parenting together after a divorce

When divorcing couples are also parents of children, no matter what the circumstances of the divorce, one fact remains: you will still be parenting together even if you are no longer a couple. Learning quickly how to work with one another effectively in your parenting roles will benefit you and—more importantly—your children.

For divorced couples this adds additional challenges to the already-difficult parenting job. Most people have specific ideas of how to parent. When a couple is bound together in love, although it's not always easy, they are able to work out their differences because of mutual interest and mutual respect. However, when a couple has divorced, the mutual interest, love, and respect may no longer be present. The key for divorced couples is to stay focused on your area of common ground:

you each love, care about, and are vitally interested in the well-being of your children. Sometimes it may feel to one of you that the other is not focused on this. Evaluating, accusing, and complaining about how the other is parenting will not help you or your children.

By now you no doubt realize that you cannot control another person, whether this other person is your child or your former spouse. The sooner you accept this and move forward, the better and more satisfying your life will be.

You cannot control whether your former spouse is too liberal with privileges, too strict with academic demands, too lenient with imposing consequences, or too severe in teaching money management. All you can control is you. This means you can control the kind of parent you are and the kind of person you are to your former spouse, your child's other parent.

When your child is present and you insult, belittle, or criticize your child's other parent, you immediately create an internal conflict for your child. If she agrees with you, then she feels she is betraying and being unloving toward her other parent. If he disagrees with you, he feels he is betraying and being unloving toward you. Children's need for love and belonging extends toward both parents. Ultimately, when you insult your former spouse, you create in your children the desire to move away from you, as they would any person who creates this kind of internal conflict for them.

The desire to hurt or get back at your former spouse may be great. But the route to such revenge, whether justified or not, is not through your children. By attempting to walk down that path, you will only succeed in driving your children further away from you, sometimes emotionally, sometimes physically, and sometimes both.

If you feel you must, the place for venting your outrage and upset over your former spouse's treatment of you is in therapy, not with your children. The simplest and most important step to successfully parenting together when you are no longer together is *never* to say anything negative about your former spouse in front of your children. Although this person is "former" to you, he or she is still your children's father or mother now and forever. No one, including your children, wants to hear anyone, even you, disparage his parents.

As much as possible, aim toward creating a process to use when you and your former spouse disagree or have differing points of view. Disagreements can make an already difficult task even more difficult. Sadly, if you could have created a process to manage your differences when you were together, then you might not have divorced. Learning this process now will still be helpful to your children.

Additional adults may now be in the picture because you have a new love, for example, or your former love has a new spouse. Here is a word of caution. Each of you can certainly consult and seek counsel from these important new people in your lives, but keep them out of the process as you and your former spouse develop a way to manage your differences. The two of you are keeping your children in the forefront of this process toward resolution. This you have in common.

Remember when you were helping two of your children work out their differences? This is the same process you two parents will use now with each other. Each of you will ask yourself, *What do I want that I am trying to get using this plan, this proposal, this answer to resolve the difficulty?* Answer these questions in private, alone. Then set a time, ideally well removed from any stress, where each of you shares your answers with the other.

Your goal at this time is to be sure you clearly understand the other person's intended outcome. Do not go any further in seeking resolution. Simply understand the desired outcome from the other person's perspective. Allow at least twenty-four hours to pass before you speak again. During this interim period, each of you should evaluate whether the other's plan or proposal is acceptable to you. If it is not, your job is to create *several* compromise plans or proposals that allow you each to get most of what you want. Independently and away from each other, create as many alternatives as you can. Now the two of you will work together to find one alternative that is acceptable to both of you.

Obviously this process is easier to read about than to put into practice. As you may recognize, it is similar to the process advocated for resolving differences you may have with your children or that your children may have with each other. That's because this is the same peaceful process that allows each person to meet his and her need for power in a mutually respectful way.

Because this peaceful process is certainly a new way for the two of you to relate to and deal with each other, try to find a very simple, almost inconsequential issue on which to practice using these guidelines. The more frequently you both practice when there is less emotion involved, the greater the chance you will be successful when you face more stressful, emotionally charged issues.

● How will you survive?

Here are some additional ideas to help you handle some of the challenges you now face as a divorced parent. Among all of your many worries and concerns, your children's emotional and financial welfare probably ranks high on your list. How will you cope? How will your children cope? How will you handle everything, including them?

Is your seven-year-old son's inability to tie his shoelaces an indication that he needs more practice with this new manual skill, or is he reverting to more childish behaviors? Is your teenage daughter's withdrawal a result of her age or of the breakup of the family? Where can you get the help and wise words of counsel you need as you face the role of single parent? Your own parents may offer some advice, but if

parenting tip

When it's nap time, spend quiet time resting yourself. When you're a single parent, it feels like there is more than twice as much that needs to be accomplished now that all chores and responsibilities are falling on you. Although it's tempting to complete all sorts of household chores during this time, now more than ever, you need to recharge your batteries too. Divorce is death. With death comes mourning. Mourning is hard work and takes more energy than you realize. This is one of the reasons you feel exhausted all of the time. So now, sit down with a book or a magazine or spend time meditating. Count your breaths and your blessings, even if you have to dig deep to find some. Turn off the television, radio, and your mind.

Quiet time, rest time, is your time to get some distance from your parenting job. Although it may feel indulgent, it is absolutely necessary to help you meet your need for freedom and contributes to your self-care that is so necessary right now. By recharging your batteries and caring for yourself, you will have more love to give your children.

they have never faced anything like this for themselves, how can they help? Does seeking outside counsel and help mean that you are an inadequate parent? Will seeking outside help be used against you?

These and many more concerns and questions are probably

flooding your consciousness. At the same time you may be preoccupied with worries of your own financial and emotional welfare. The early days of divorce, as your reality changes, may feel overwhelming. Daily chores that you previously shared with your spouse now fall solely on your shoulders to complete. They may seem like one more burden that you cannot handle on your own.

You have less energy and reserve to deal with your children's bickering with you and each other. Is it your imagination, or are your children bickering and arguing more frequently? Perhaps you are fantasizing about hiding under the blankets in your bed, waiting to come out when everything is all better. When will that be? How can you begin to improve and do better when you are feeling so alone and frightened? And then you find yourself facing the holiday season that begins with Halloween and doesn't end until after Valentine's Day. All of these celebrations seem steeped in family time and celebrations of love. Do you still have a family?

Divorce means death. Your family, as you and your children have known it, is dying. You and your children are grieving and experiencing deep mourning. The first stage of the grieving process is shock and denial. This is characterized by feeling lost and overwhelmed. You have no energy or ability to cope with what is expected and normal. The unexpected seems to crop up almost daily now. You may feel completely ill-equipped and inadequate to handle anything alone.

● Helping your children cope

Despite the emotional turmoil you are feeling, you are not the only person dealing with these seemingly overwhelming changes. As a parent, your life includes your children. Their emotional roller coaster is not the same as yours, but it is no less upsetting and difficult to bear.

Children have less experience and maturity to help them understand what is happening to their family and to cope with their own emotional experiences. For your children, the answer to the question of how to cope lies with their parents. For their parents, this new parenting process can offer some answers.

Your psychological need for safety and security drives you to create a home for yourself and your children. As you and your children begin to face the changes caused by divorce in your family, your very foundation of safety and security feels shaky. Your children's worries and fears also include losing parental love. They wonder *Am I safe? Where will I live? If Mom and Dad don't love each other anymore, do they still love me?*

Children need their parents to give them a sense of safety and security. This started at birth when you first held and comforted your crying child. You provided the feelings of safety and security to your children through your hugs and kisses. Over time, children count on their parents as the primary people to help them follow and meet their needs for safety and love. Divorce threatens all they have ever known because the people, relationships, and routines they have always counted on to meet their basic psychological needs for safety and love are changing.

Children learned to believe that parents frightened away the bogey man and chased monsters out from under their beds. When they were injured, your soft words and tender ministering provided the cure just as magically as bandages could. You created a sense of safety and security for your children as you developed daily routines, habits, and rituals. Now that change is expected or happening, your children are feeling less safe and secure. As a result, you may be inundated with questions or complaints from your child as daily routines are altered or are threatened.

● Rituals and routines

Divorce is a very unfamiliar situation that you and your child are facing. Your child is looking to you to provide a sense of safety and security, especially during these uncertain times. The unknown means the unexpected, unanticipated, and potentially unsafe. Your job to provide a secure environment may be made easier if you use these simple suggestions.

Maintain daily routines and rituals, even through the holidays. You may not feel you have the energy or interest, but this is vital for your child's peace of mind. Seeing the familiar Halloween skeleton you have always put on the front door helps your child know that in spite of the upheaval in your family, he can count on you to keep his life steady. As hard and challenging as it may seem, putting up all of the Christmas or winter holiday ornaments tells your child that some parts of life are changing, but some parts will remain constant. By decking the halls, which may be the very last thing you are interested in doing, you are telling your child that he is loved and can feel safe in the familiar and usual holiday celebrations.

Whether this has been part of your previous ritual or not, begin each day talking with your children about the day's schedule and plans. When you provide your children with information about the day's events, you allow them to know what to expect during this time that seems filled with so many unpleasant surprises. End each day talking with your children, whether they are with you or with their other parent. Connect at the end of your day just to say "I love you" so that your child can feel safe in the knowledge that his family may be changing but the love of his parents is permanent.

When you are not with your child, tell her where you are, what you are doing, and what she can expect, including when she can expect to see you again. Give her a photograph of you or, better yet, a photograph of both you and your child together. Make a copy for yourself. It is important that you both feel connected with each other even during those times you are not physically together. It would be a good idea for

parenting tip

 When you're parenting alone, consider letting your children help you with some of the tasks you've been doing, like making school lunches. I usually made my boys' lunches in the evening when I was cleaning up after dinner. It just became habit and routine. But at some point each boy began to give more specific instructions for what he wanted for his lunch. "I want oranges sliced into wedges," one child would request while the other might request oranges sliced as smiles. Sometimes a request was made for peanut butter and jelly while other times a cheese sandwich with mustard was ordered.

Eventually it dawned on me that if the boys were so clear about what they wanted to eat, as well as how they wanted their fruit sliced, then perhaps it was time for them to help me. Without a great deal of fuss or fanfare, that is exactly what happened. Each evening after our family meal, I would begin to put the next day's lunches together. And by turn, each boy would be my helper. From there we progressed until each made his own lunch for the following day.

your child to have a picture of her other parent, too, for the very same reason.

As overwhelming and difficult as these strange days feel, do the best you can to maintain routines and rituals. This might include creating new ones as your life continues to evolve. For example altering where you live or the days you spend together may require you to craft some new rituals. If you and your children have not previously followed

peaceful parenting quiz

Which of the following do you think would help you keep your resolution not to say anything nasty or demeaning about your former spouse?

Your children come back from a weekend visiting their father. Each child is furious about the dad's behavior for different reasons. Each has told you in private and then together that they think he is losing his mind, unfair, and unreasonable and that neither wants to see or visit him ever again. What do you do?

● Ask each child to give you more information. Do your best to solicit explicit details. Call your lawyer if you need to and arrange to alter child custody to keep the children with you, the practice of eating at least one family meal together when they're with you, start this now. Research indicates that eating a family meal together is the single most important routine that parents can establish to help their children succeed in school and in life. At this time, eating at least one meal together is even more important to help you and your children feel safe, secure, and connected with each other.

The early days of shock, denial, and overwhelmed emotions will

honoring their wishes not to visit their father.

● Listen as each child shares his or her story with you. Once each has vented, ask them how they plan to resolve the problems with their father. Do they want to call and talk with him before their next visit?

● Ask friends for the name of a good therapist. Connect the children with a professional to help them learn to deal with their father without you. You are working with your therapist to keep from saying anything negative about your former spouse.

The answer you want to avoid is the first. Although this may be your temptation, you will gain nothing by having children who are not able to develop a positive relationship with their father. He will always be their father, so they will always have a relationship. They need help learning how to make this relationship good and positive. If your own upset and anger make you unable to help your children learn how to develop this relationship with their father, then get them professional help.

give way to other challenges and changes. You and your children are not through all of the adjustments that are needed following a divorce, but by maintaining rituals and routines during the early days and stages, you and your children will all feel better daily. You will each feel safer and be able to maintain your bond, which is vital for everyone's well-being.

● Conclusion

Although a divorce is the death of your family as you and your children have known it, your job is to help your children realize that these changes will ultimately work out for everyone's benefit. This means that you need to take care of yourself, your children, and the new, negotiated relationship you are creating with your former spouse.

Although you cannot control anyone else's behavior, you can control your own. That means that every day you will work to create an environment where you and your children can meet your needs for safety, love, power, fun, and freedom. When connecting with your former spouse about anything that needs to be negotiated, create plans ahead of time for ways that you can be safe, loving, powerful, and free. Plan ahead to create ways for your former spouse to be able to meet his or her needs for safety, love, power, and freedom around you.

Resolve to never say anything negative about your former spouse in front of your children. Maintain this resolution even if your former spouse does not offer you the same courtesy. Although this resolution may take time and practice, if you can achieve it, your children will always be grateful to you.

parenting

Q *My oldest daughter, Jana, who's six, wants to eat all the time. Even after she has just finished eating a meal, she comes to me less than an hour later telling me she is hungry, asking for a snack or a treat. This all began after her father and I split up. Because of my guilt and worry about ending my marriage, I gave her food without hesitation. But now I'm worried that something is wrong and I am resisting her requests for food. Her pediatrician assures me that there is no physical problem. Is it possible that she and I are in a power struggle? Or do you think she is using food to try to fill the emotional hole created by her father's absence?*

A I suspect that Jana is as hungry as she claims, only not for food. I also suspect that the more you and she engage in a tug of war over food, the greater the tension that exists in your relationship will grow. Although this feels like a power struggle between you, I think Jana needs more love and belonging, a greater connection between ▶

parenting
Q&A

the two of you. Probably this is because the only family she has known has changed.

Now that you are parenting alone, you may have less time and attention to give Jana. Many household chores and responsibilities that before were accomplished by two adults must now be completed only by you. Jana may misinterpret this diminished amount of time together as meaning she has less of your love and nurturing. From Jana's point of view, she is feeling less secure, less sure of what is happening now and of what is going to happen to her family. What appears to you to be Jana's increased demand for more power, a power struggle, may actually be her increased demand for loving, nurturing, and a sense of safety and well-being. She may in fact get less of your attention because she is capable of completing self-caring tasks independently, and at the same time you now have more worries and simply more to do. She may not be able to think of another way to request more love, connection, and security than by asking to be fed.

Here's what I suggest. If you are presently making any comment when Jana asks for more food, stop. Even though you are frightened about her gaining weight, when she requests more food, offer her a reasonable snack without commenting at all.

The other suggestion I have is that you ask Jana to help you plan and prepare family meals. Sit down with her and make the menu for the week. When you grocery shop, ask Jana which items she wants to be responsible for finding from the grocery list. Engage and connect with her about food in a positive, celebratory, privileged way. Menu planning, meal preparation, and serving can become activities for special bonding for the two of you to cultivate together. You could also use a helper right about now.

Finally, about an hour after dinner is served, just before Jana ordinarily comes to you requesting a snack or food, seek her out. Ask her for a hug. Tell her you miss her and want a little loving, special time with her. Suggest that the two of you read a short story or sing a song together. Whatever you choose to do, it doesn't need to be anything big or dramatic. You are aiming for regularly and consistently feeding her with some extra love, affection, and nonfood nurturing.

It is extremely important that you practice all three of these steps at the same time. Don't forget to eliminate any verbal commentary you are making about her eating habits. Even though it may be difficult to stop what you are doing, make sure to regularly seek her out and give her your love, attention, and hugs. And see if you and she can begin working as a gourmet team, creating meals together. Concocting your fun and love together with food planning, preparing, and enjoying will most likely change the food struggle you are presently in with Jana.

 Epilogue

The absolutely foolproof plan for successful parenting

The father of a six-year-old first grader was concerned because Charlie, his gentle, easygoing, friendly son, had befriended the classroom bully. The bully, a larger child than the others in his class, did not bully or attempt to control Charlie. But the bully did prevent all of the other children from getting too close or becoming friends with Charlie. This child wanted to keep Charlie to himself. Charlie's parents had even considered taking him out of this school and sending him to another. What should he and his wife do? this dad wanted to know.

To better understand this situation, I needed more answers from this father. Was Charlie unhappy with this friendship? Did Charlie feel as if he was being isolated from other children he might want to play with or make friends with? Or was Charlie the type of kind and sympathetic child who saw this other child's isolation and sought him out? If that was the case, it was more than likely that sending Charlie to another school would only result in Charlie finding the isolated bully-like child in that class. Did Charlie have an opportunity to play with other children at some time during his school day and on weekends? During class times, did the teacher help Charlie pair with other children? Did the teacher pair the "bully" with other children? Had the child's parents had any conferences or conversations with this teacher? Had the parents had any conversation with Charlie?

As it turned out, Charlie's parents had discussed the situation with Charlie's teacher. "She is a very experienced, seasoned teacher," his father told me. "She really seemed to understand immediately, sharing with us that she had observed what we were talking about. She also reassured us that she would continue to monitor the situation and intervene appropriately."

Then what did this father want from me? I asked him just that. "I'm not really sure," he admitted to me. "Last week I was on the telephone with my sister who is a first-grade teacher. I was worried that perhaps Charlie wasn't being challenged enough academically. After talking with her, I finished the conversation worried that perhaps Charlie wasn't going to be able to keep up academically."

Finally, I was beginning to understand this father's concern. Perhaps you can relate. With each passing year, our children are maturing and growing. They are becoming increasingly independent from us. Will they be okay? Are they prepared? Have we done all we can to help them? Are we doing enough? Are we doing too much?

"Parenting our children is a hard job, isn't it?" I asked this father.

"It really is," he admitted to me with relief. "It is much harder than I ever thought. I was the youngest of my parents' six children. How did they do it?"

Now we were at the heart of this father's worries and concerns. As parents, you want to do the best job you can for your children. But what does that mean? How do you know what is best? Will it be too late if you realize that what you did may not have been the best for your child?

Here it is, the absolutely foolproof plan for successful parenting that all parents are already capable of completing. If you follow this advice, I guarantee it will help you and your child. Ready?

Step 1: Every day, tell your child that you love her. When you see her for the first time in the morning, wish her a good morning and tell her you love her. When you bid her good-bye as you each go to your daily routine, tell her you love her. When you greet her again in the evening, smile and tell her that you love her. When you tuck her into bed at night, wish her a good night and tell her that you love her. Smile from your heart and generously share your love for her in word and deed. For a few moments during the day and evening when you are apart, conjure up your child's beautiful face and remember that you love her.

Step 2: Every day, laugh and play often. Take time out and get away from all of those important adult tasks on your to-do list that you need to complete during your day, evening, and weekend, and play a silly game, read a good book—do something! Laugh and play with your child lots and lots and lots.

Too many of us grew up following our parents' admonition, "You can't go and play until you get all of your chores done." As children, most of us were capable of completing our chores with time left over to play. Now, as an adult, are you waiting to play with your child until you get your work done? Do not wait. You will never get all of your work done. That's part of what it means to be an adult. But your child will not be a child forever. He is not going to be waiting around for you to get your chores done. Instead, laugh and play with him now, and then he can help you complete some of your work.

Ten years after your child has left home, you won't even remember what the chore or work was that you put off so you could play a game; sing a goofy song; and spend more time laughing, relaxing, and playing. But ten years after your child leaves home, you both will remember the love, laughter, and play.

That is the complete, absolute foolproof plan for successful parenting that you are already capable of completing. Can you do it? Of course you can! Will you do it? I hope so.

 Appendix A

Tried-and-true parenting tricks

While presenting peaceful parenting ideas to people in North America, Australia, New Zealand, Singapore, and Bogotá, Columbia, I learned many tips and ideas that can bring more fun and love to family life. Here are a few I think you will enjoy and find helpful.

All of these activities are designed to provide enjoyable ways for you and your child to problem solve and bond at the same time. You can use these ideas as a starting point to brainstorm your own ideas too.

● Special alone time

Ever since one mother's children were young, she would arrange to have special alone time once a week with each child. The ideas and activities ranged from a visit to the local zoo or a game of cards to a trip to the public library to choose books for the week. They never ran out of ideas. What was most important was having Mom concentrate all of her attention on only that one child at least once a week.

What I didn't know then, but have realized now that my children are teenagers, is how important that ritual was, not only during their childhood, but especially when they became teenagers and young adults. The kinds of activities changed as the children grew older. But because we had established this routine early, we continue to have an ongoing foundation for time to connect.

Many teenagers can't find time to spend with their mothers. This mother established special alone time with her children so that her teenagers thought it was no big deal even during their adolescent years. If Mom had something specific she wanted to discuss with either child, she knew she had an established and appropriate time already set aside. Mostly their time has been spent having fun and enjoying each other's company.

When the children were small, they felt special having their mother exclusively to themselves. Now that the children are young adults, their mother feels special knowing each child will make time for her.

● Build an indoor maze

This is especially fun during winter or rainy months when being housebound feels boring and tedious. Gather blankets, clothespins, and large boxes (save some especially for this adventure). Using only the rooms parents designate as "safe," cover furniture with the blankets to make tents and tunnels for passageways and use the boxes to create a fort or castle. All who enter this maze must maneuver through the various spaces by crawling.

● Whisper

About an hour before you begin your evening bedtime routine, ask everyone to begin whispering to each other. If the television, radio, or any other electronic device is making noise, turn the volume down very low. Lower the lights. You are winding down the sights and sounds of the day, creating a subdued environment and indicating that the day is coming to a calm and peaceful end.

● Monthly celebrations

As part of an effort to eliminate rewarding children for good behavior, institute a monthly celebration. On the last Sunday of the month, celebrate all of the positive events that have happened to each member of the family during that month. You could make a picnic lunch to eat at a playground or park or go to a local fast-food place or make a pizza dinner at home with a special dessert. Try to do something different each month. Create a "celebration box" by decorating a container. This is where you will collect ideas about what is to be celebrated each month. Whenever anything worth celebrating happens to any family member, write it down and place it in the celebration box. This might include an improved math test score, someone finding his lost watch, someone getting a job promotion, or someone winning a tennis or soccer game. The items can be large and significant or just a moment worth noting. During the monthly celebration, read the accomplishments and respond with appropriate applause and cheers from all. The more you begin to collect and notice, the more you will realize there is much to celebrate.

● Morning map

Help your young child navigate her morning routine by drawing a map of her morning together. Step 1 is a picture of your child eating breakfast; step 2, brushing her teeth; step 3, getting dressed; step 4, packing her backpack; step 5, the child is walking out the door waving good-bye. Hang this map in a place where your child can easily see and refer to it. Now your morning routine can be transformed to one that involves asking your child to refer to her morning map rather than you nagging and cajoling her into completing morning tasks.

● What do actions teach?

When your child fails to complete a task or chore that he has committed to, ask him, "What did you just teach me about you?" Some parents have found that this decreases the excuses their child gives for why he didn't do what had been agreed to. One parent has found that this helps her child understand that the child's lack of follow-through has a consequence. Although the consequence may be different from what the child intended, his behavior does affect other people who were counting on him and on their relationships. As a result of asking this question, one mother found her child doing a better job in keeping and following through with commitments he made. She also asked this question when her son successfully handled his responsibilities, showing that positive behaviors have consequences too.

● Restaurant memory game

After orders have been placed and while everyone is waiting for food to arrive, try this.

1. Everyone look very carefully at the table.
2. One person closes his eyes and another person changes the place setting, either by taking something away, adding something, or changing the pattern.
3. The person with closed eyes opens them and tries to detect the change.

   Now switch who closes his eyes and play again.

Tooth fairy twist

Here is a new twist for your children and the tooth fairy. Ask your child to leave a note for the fairy along with her tooth. Then have the tooth fairy leave a book as well as a written response instead of money.

Magic spray

When your young child is afraid of monsters and other frightening apparitions during the night, protect him with an anti-monster spray bottle. Some parents fill colorful spray bottles with "power" that their child can use at night, when needed. One family told me they went on-line and found a company that sells them. Whichever magic spray you choose, be sure to have your child work with you in choosing the most powerful color and filling it with all the power and safety necessary to keep your child safe when alone in his bed during the night.

Helping hands

One first-grade teacher asks the parents of her students to trace their own hands on colored paper and then cut them out. She asks the parents to write a short note or poem or message on the paper hands. Each child carries his or her parents' helping hands in a gallon-sized plastic bag. This allows children to go to school while staying in touch with and connected to their parents.

● The what would you do? game

Initially, this game was created by a parent to help her children develop good manners. Now she uses it to help her children clarify ethics too:

1. Prior to playing the game, create several questions that you will put to the family group. Here are some examples of questions for the game:
    What would you do if someone cut in front of you in line?
    What would you do if someone wanted to copy your homework answers?
    What would you do if you discovered your favorite toy was missing after your best friend came to your house to play?
    What would you do if you were eating dinner at a friend's house and someone at the table burped out loud?
2. Ask each person to share and explain her answer.
3. People can disagree with each other's answers, but no answer should be considered incorrect or wrong. Everyone is encouraged to share a story that exemplifies a real-life experience of the question.

● The loud game

When your children are inside the house and being too noisy, you can try playing the loud game. Go outside with the children and ask them to be as loud as possible with you. You might ask them to skip, hop, sing, or dance with you while being loud. Carry on for a bit of time. Then ask them if they have gotten all of the loudness out of their system. If not, go for another round of raucous singing and dancing. If they say yes, ask the children if they can leave their noise outside and go back inside with you and be more quiet. Once back inside, everyone will be quieter and more tired. If the volume starts to creep back up, ask the children to go outside again and get rid of their loudness.

● The echo game

One mother created this game to help her children become better listeners. Choose a poem, limerick, riddle, story from a book or magazine, or something from your imagination. It is best to have the material written down. The sillier the poem or verse the better.

1. Choose one person to be the reader.
2. The reader reads only the first word of a sentence from the chosen material.
3. Each player takes a turn repeating or echoing what the reader has said.
4. The reader reads the first and second word from the chosen reading material.
5. Each player takes a turn repeating what the reader has said.
6. The reader reads the first, second, and third word from the material.
7. Each player takes a turn repeating what the reader has said.
8. Play continues on in this manner. Players are eliminated whenever a player echoes incorrectly what the reader has read. The person who can repeat the most words wins and becomes the next reader.

● Table talk

Set the timer at the dinner table if you have more than one child who needs and wants to tell of his day's events. Each child is given ten minutes (or an age-appropriate amount) of solo time to tell his stories and day's adventures to the family. Different days of the week can be designated for who will have the first turn to share his day, the second, and so forth.

● Indoor camping pajama day

One family's experience during a power outage from an ice storm led to this game. The family pretended they were camping. Everyone stayed in their warm pajamas all day; ate cold cereal; played board games; ate granola bars and drank juice for a snack; and stayed huddled together for comfort, warmth, and entertainment. Now the family deliberately plays this game. Nothing can be used if it requires electricity. Even though the power has not been lost, pretending there is no electricity is part of the fun.

● Settling down

Want to help a child learn to focus when she is having difficulty listening? Ask the child to use her glitter bottle (instructions follow) to settle down. Ask the child to shake her bottle and tell her this represents her—all full of energy, feeling scattered and all shook up. Then ask her to watch as the glitter settles to the bottom of the bottle. The child can see the peace in the bottle. Help the child focus on the feelings of calm and quiet that are settling in her body just as the glitter is doing in her bottle.

• Glitter bottle

To do this little project you will need a clear, empty bottle (a small plastic soda or water bottle with a flat lid will work), water, glitter or metallic snowflakes, and glue to help your child make her own glitter and snowflake bottle.

1. Using a funnel (a homemade one will do), fill the bottle about one quarter full with glitter.
2. Fill the bottle with water.
3. Glue the cap onto the top of the bottle. Allow the glue to set before use.
4. Shake the bottle, turn it upside down, and watch the storm begin.

• Convenient baby calendar

Instead of using an expensive and time-consuming baby book to capture your child's growth and milestone achievements, use a regular wall calendar. Each day record something new about your child's development or a newly learned skill or memorable moment that brought a smile to your face or joy to your heart. Although it may not be as lovely as a baby book, it is more convenient and handy during the first busy and hectic year of your child's life.

 Appendix B

A more in-depth look at certain peaceful parenting solutions

H ere are some ideas and answers to additional questions as well as stories of success I have accumulated from people all over the world.

• Communicating with your teen

If you want your reluctant, private teenager to open up and confide in you more, decrease the frequency of your judgments and criticisms. A mother of a teenage daughter felt as though her daughter was holding back from her and not talking. The first step that helped was that this mother made the effort to learn more about her daughter's normal and expected development. Teenagers want and need more power and freedom. This mother also began to understand that perhaps her

220 • HOW TO BE A GREAT PARENT

daughter perceived Mom's questions as attempts to pry and invade her privacy. Now this mother has changed her ways. She asks her daughter an additional question when they talk: "If you knew I wasn't going to criticize or judge you, what would you tell me?" This has dramatically changed the conversation between mother and daughter. As a result, the daughter is now sharing more with her mom. Mom now realizes that she was criticizing and judging more than she realized, keeping her daughter from feeling safe to share information and ideas with her mother. With the criticism and judgment gone, their relationship is thriving.

● Evaluating your own behavior as a parent

As the parent of a teenager, you are faced with the thrill and dilemma of your child's maturation and desire for increased freedom. If all is well, you have taught your child the skills necessary for him to handle the big wide world without you. But how do you know if all is well? You may be reassured by how your child behaves in your presence, but how do you know what he does when you are not around? You may even feel confident in your own child's skills, abilities, and demonstrated maturity in handling increasing freedoms. But what about the other teenagers with whom your child spends time? Can you trust them? Can you trust that the parents of other children have done a good job too? It is difficult to trust your child when he is a teenager, even when you have worked to build that trust for so many years.

How will your children ever learn to handle themselves without you if you are always around? At some point, as frightening as it may be to you, you must let go, at least a little bit, so your children can learn how to fly without you. As long as you stay involved and connected with your child, you should also trust he will come to you if he gets into difficulty or runs into a problem.

That said, parents still have a tremendous desire to check up on what their son or daughter is up to. This curiosity and desire to keep their child safe may lead some parents to pry or spy on their child. Recently a friend told me she found a letter in her son's room that was sent to him by a girl. This mom did not deliberately set out to spy on her son but was returning clean laundry to his room and came upon the letter.

Driven by curiosity, she spent some time trying to rationalize why opening his private letter would be okay. She was also suspicious of her own motivation and called me for advice.

"Is what you are thinking about doing going to improve your relationship?" As soon as I asked my friend this question, she knew she must walk away from her son's letter, unopened.

During adolescence your children crave increased privacy, which helps them feel a greater sense of power and freedom. As your children guard their privacy, you grow increasingly suspicious and fearful. But if you let these suspicions and fears lead to breaking into your children's private letters, e-mails, and phone calls, what will that do to your relationship? Here are three solutions that may help:

1. Choose to trust your child. Trusting is a choice. As difficult as that may be, if you don't trust your children, how will you ever teach them that they are trustworthy?
2. Talk with your child about her life, interests, friends, hopes, dreams, disappointments, and so on. Be prepared for your child to be guarded and suspicious of your interest. But don't let that stop you from showing that you care and want to know what is happening and important in her life.
3. Ask yourself, *Is what I'm about to do or say going to improve our relationship?* If the answer is no, then don't do it or say it. If the answer is, you're not sure, then ask your child what effect your asking the

question or making the statement will have on your relationship. If the answer is that it will improve your relationship, then say it or do it.

No one said being a parent was easy. Perhaps no one ever told you about the fears that go along with parenting. During the frightening time of parenting an adolescent, you can maneuver your way more successfully by evaluating your own behaviors. If you do, you have a greater chance of keeping your children in a positive, loving relationship with you.

Eventually they grow older; their privacy is less guarded. In fact, they will probably look forward to sharing their lives with you. They will have learned you trusted them. And you will have demonstrated that you were trustworthy.

● Homework autonomy

Using self-evaluation questions can transform homework time at your house. Although this process is best used at the beginning of a new school year, this parent began at the end of the school year and still found success. The process will work whenever you engage your child in owning his own homework responsibility.

One parent explained to her daughter that her homework was her job. Teachers gave work to help her learn all that was necessary for the fourth grade. Because this child's days were spent in school, she better understood what teachers wanted her to learn by completing her homework assignments.

Next, this parent asked her daughter if she was willing to learn all that she could. The daughter agreed that this was something that she wanted. This was the start of developing a plan to make sure the daughter could spend the necessary time on her schoolwork as well as have time to do all the other activities she liked to do during her evenings. When the daughter returned home from school each day, together parent and daughter would review all the homework assigned and the daughter's guess for the time needed, and they would list all the other activities the daughter wanted to do during her evening. Parent and child created a schedule.

Next they discussed and evaluated the best place for doing homework, designating a place that allowed her to concentrate the best, so that she could get her homework done efficiently and well. This gave the daughter more free time for her other planned activities.

After following the new plan for a few weeks, the parent asked her daughter to self-evaluate the time she was putting into her homework. Was it enough? Was she learning all that she could or was she simply getting through? Was she interested in giving one subject or one assignment more effort? What did she want to achieve from completing her homework?

The first year of following this process was instructive. By the following year, this child spontaneously planned and then informed her mother of her evening plans. She also shared with her mother the assignments she really wanted to concentrate on.

• Rewarding may be counterproductive

Although it is currently a common practice by teachers in schools and child-care centers, rewarding our children for behaving the way we want them to is contrary to our children's nature and peaceful parenting. As you may have already experienced in your own life, not only does this type of external reward or bribe not work over the long haul, it may in fact be counterproductive. A child may stop working with or for you unless he can negotiate some kind of reward from you. Extensive research exists indicating that rewards eventually decrease the kind of behavior desired.

Offering rewards or bribes becomes a power struggle between parent and child. If the child does what you ask because of the promised reward, and this is contrary to what the child wants, he feels powerless—as if you have exerted power over him. If the child feels powerless, over time he may purposely defy your wishes as his way of meeting his need for power. Or he may realize he can control you by refusing to do what you ask unless you offer a reward or a bribe. Who is really in charge? You will find that instead of the two of you working issues out together, you are spending your time struggling to meet your needs for power over one another.

How can you determine if this is true about your relationship with your child? Ask yourself if most of your conversations fall into the if-then category:

> If you behave well at the grocery store, then we will eat lunch at your favorite restaurant.
>
> If you do your homework now, then you can watch television after dinner.
>
> If you eat all of your dinner, then you can have dessert.

In all of these circumstances the parent is trying to control and have power over the child's behavior by bribing or promising a reward.

The other common use of rewards is connecting a child's behavior to earning a sticker. When a certain number of stickers are earned, the child gets to convert these stickers into a special prize. Initially these programs seem to work, with a child changing her behavior as requested by her parent. She may even earn the special prize. But as many parents have discovered, eventually the child stops cooperating, no matter how wonderful the bribe. Eventually she wants to follow her internal drive for power more than she wants whatever prize is promised.

What can parents do instead? Together you and your child can set up something fun for you to do after you complete a chore without attaching any behavioral expectations or stipulations to the activity. For instance, "After we complete the grocery shopping, then we can go eat lunch at McDonald's." This is not setting up a reward because you will go out to lunch no matter how your child behaves in the grocery store. Instead of rewarding your child for a good report card, hold a celebratory dinner no matter what kind of grades she received to signify reaching another milestone. Deciding with your child that you will visit the local park after he cleans his room gives him something to look forward to as he performs a job that may not be his favorite.

Although this may sound like a difference in semantics, it is much more than that. The difference is that you are not exerting power over your child by making the fun time be dependent upon him performing as you want him to. If the two of you decide on some fun activity to do following a task or chore, do not dangle this activity as a reward that is contingent upon your child's performance. That is exercising your power over him. Instead, the two of you can decide together what you would enjoy doing together after a task that is less than fun has been completed.

If your child decides he wants to establish a reward system, put him in charge of developing the program and evaluating whether or not he has earned a sticker by completing the job to his standard. The difference is he is in charge, he has the power, and you are the partner supporting his effort.

Why not try eliminating any rewards or bribes you have already established? When you do, your child may surprise you and complete her chores, jobs, and tasks on her own, feeling proud of herself with a greater sense of internal power.

• Discord between child and partner

I often receive questions like this one: My child and fiancé don't get along. It feels as though they are playing tug-of-war over me. What can I do? My advice would be to leave them alone. As long as you continue to take one person's side over the other's, the two of them will probably continue their contest to see who can win your approval. But if you refuse to take either side, insisting the two of them come up with a solution together, you will remove yourself from being the prize they are both fighting over.

This is the same recommendation I have made to parents of two or more children who are arguing. When parents take one child's side over another's, children will continue to argue, seeing who can gain more power by winning their parents' approval. In this case, your fiancé and child are engaged in the same struggle.

However, in your situation you can take advantage of a big difference between the two situations. Your fiancé is an adult, so you need to ask for his help. Explain to him what you have observed between him and your child. Explain to him that you see the two of them engaging in battles to win your approval and attention. Explain to him that you do not want to be placed in a position where you must choose one over the other and that you plan to remove yourself from the situations where he and your child are arguing and asking you to intervene. Tell him that you plan to ask the two of them to work disagreements out together.

At this point you need to listen to find out what is going on from your fiancé's point of view. It could be that he is trying to position himself in a more parental role than he had before you became engaged. After all, when he made the commitment of marriage, he also made the commitment to co-parent your child. He may feel he needs to exert more power in that role than he did when he was your boyfriend. If this is true, then the two of you need to make a plan to help him move in the direction of gaining some authority. Now he is trying to do this through bickering and arguing. Help him find a better way.

It would also be a good idea to have a private and separate discussion with your child. Although I suspect your child is in a competitive phase of his development, it still would be a good idea to ask him if he has noticed that he and your fiancé seem to be arguing and bickering. Ask him how he wants to get along with your fiancé. Explain to him that your quality world picture is seeing the two of them getting along and working their differences out. Share with him your dream of what your family will be like together, after the marriage. Ask him to share with you any dreams he has.

Finally, it may be helpful to ask your fiancé to plan outings and special times when he and your child can enjoy one another without you. These don't need to be big events like camping for a weekend, but more simple kinds of outings, like going to the playground together or to the park or the zoo. At first they may be together for only an hour or so. They could plan to make something special for you as a surprise. Anything at all would do the trick as long as they are working and spending time together without you. The purpose of this time is for them to get to know and enjoy each other, to learn how to have fun without you. If you're not there, then they can't argue over you, and if they have disagreements, they will have to work out a solution together.

● Redefining expectations

One mother wrote to me with this plea for help: I have one daughter who is perfect, caring about neatness and being responsible. It is easy to be her parent. My younger daughter is my challenge. She is chaotic, irresponsible, messy, and forgetful. I try to help her, making lists and insisting she empty her school backpack with me. Help please!

It's easy to parent a child who has similar quality world pictures to your own. Sometimes a parent shares similar pictures with one child, and as a result there are fewer conflicts between the parent and this child. Sometimes a parent's "difficult" child seems that way because this child's quality world pictures are different from the parent's.

For instance, suppose you and your "easy" or "perfect" child share similar ideas and values about order and neatness in your environment. But your "difficult" or "challenging" child may be messy and chaotic. How to cope?

Even for the messy, chaotic child there is an order and pattern that suits her needs. It's just that this pattern is different from what suits you and your needs. In fact, the "difficult" child sees her parent as the one who is difficult and a challenge to her! You want to impose a certain order onto her environment, and this is different from how she wants things. From your child's perspective she is feeling as though she constantly has to accommodate and change to suit you.

If you ask her to make a list and empty her backpack in an attempt to help her get organized, your child does not feel helped. Instead she feels like she is being criticized and bossed into changing so you feel better. From your child's point of view, your orderly life feels rigid.

Neither the mother nor her child has it wrong. They just have different ideas about how chaotic, orderly, free-flowing, or organized their lives should be.

What you need to do in cases like this is work together to create ideas you both can live with. This means life may be messier than you would like and more rigid than your daughter would like. You are both going to need to compromise to accommodate each other's style and point of view.

Start with the most important aspect of your complaint list. Is it the mess in the shared family space that you would most like changed? Find time during the week when you and your daughters and any other members of the household can have a meeting. At this time tell your daughters you want to come to an agreed-upon picture of how you want the family room to look. Listen to everyone's point of view, and communicate your own ideas.

Then ask the girls to work with you to come up with an agreed-upon understanding of how the room will look so you can all live with it and agree to its condition. Make a plan for how you will achieve this together. Ask each girl how you should handle it if she leaves her stuff in a heap. Ask the girls what you should do if you find dirty dishes left behind. In other words, anticipate the potential difficulties and work out a plan to handle these problems ahead of time. Plan for a follow-up meeting a week later. Continue this process for as long as it takes until you are all feeling successful about your plans and achievements.

In addition, give your "messy" daughter her own space to keep in the condition she wants (within reasonable limits). In other words, don't insist that she keep her bedroom completely picked up and spotless, with her bed made, all toys put away, and so on. This just isn't her style. If you allow her space of her own to keep in the state of order or chaos that suits her, she will be more willing to work with you and the family in maintaining the family's ideas of order in the family room.

When you feel tempted to make lists for her, first ask her if she wants your help. Then ask her if making lists for her is helpful. If she is having difficulties such as forgetting assignments, library book returns, and so on, ask her if she needs your help in solving the problem. Ask her what her plan is for solving the problem. Making lists may be a solution that works for you, but it may not be her style or plan. However, this does not mean you don't intervene at all. Simply ask her for direction in how you can help her.

Finally, stop labeling one child as your "challenge" and one as your "perfect" child. Although this is probably not your intention, by comparing your children so that one comes out on top, the other will perceive herself as being on the bottom.

Just imagine that one of your daughters told you that her father was the perfect parent and that you are the challenging, difficult parent. How would you feel? Your daughters are different, each perfect in her own way.

● Language, labels, and results

Imagine a woman who has a clear idea of what she wants. She works diligently, attempting resourceful alternative strategies to achieve her goal. She is not easily discouraged, nor does she give up, even after many unsuccessful attempts.

How might you label this woman?

How about if you learned that this is a young girl, not a woman? Would that change your label? I bet bullheaded, stubborn, and ornery were not how you described this woman. And yet, these are often the labels given to children who persist in various ways trying to get what they want.

Here's another one. Imagine a man who knows what he likes. His taste is discriminating, choosing only those possessions that feel the best and food that tastes the best and satisfies him the most. He is un-yielding, unwilling to go along with others' opinions just to put them at ease. He does not make a big deal or drama about holding out for what he wants. He is just clear.

What is your label for this man?

How does the label change when you discover that this is not a man but a two-year-old boy? Often this type of child is called picky and willful.

Amazing, isn't it?

Finally, you meet a relative of a good friend. But this person is very different from your friend. This person doesn't seem nearly as goal ori-ented or worried about pleasing others. This person's focus seems to be more on having a good time and making everything fun. You might wonder how this person and your friend could possibly come from the same family because they are so different. Do you like the achievement-oriented relative better? You might be relieved to meet the more relaxed, social relative. Whom do you think you might rather spend time with? Would your answer differ depending on the circumstances? Whom would you prefer to have at your party? Whom would you prefer to work with on your committee?

Now imagine these two people are not friends, but are your number-one and number-two children. How does your opinion change? How does comparing one child with the other affect your relationship with either child? How does comparing affect the child's relationship with his sibling? Or his own self-image?

Words are powerful. For each individual, words are full of meaning, pictures, and opinions. The words you use to describe your children to someone else or even to yourself affect your image and opinions of your children's strengths and assets as well as their shortcomings and challenges. When your children hear your descriptions of them, it also affects how they see themselves, their own opinions of themselves.

What are the words you use when describing your children? Can you see how calling your child willful, bullheaded, or "difficult" describes only one side of the picture? What opinion do you imagine your child forms of himself when he hears these labels?

These very behaviors may be assets that will serve your child well in the future. Your bullheaded daughter may persist as an adult when she is pursuing her career goals. A child who is not a people pleaser but who is clear about what she wants may be less likely to accept the influence of her friends to drink alcohol during her teen years.

Start to listen to the labels and language you use. Spend time figuring out another way to describe your child's behaviors that includes both the positive aspects as well as the irritating or negative. Watch to see if changing the labels you use changes your opinion and picture of your child. How does changing your opinion and picture of your child affect your child's behavior?

For a final challenge, practice this process on yourself. What are the labels you use to describe yourself? What are the results? Do you call yourself lazy? Is contemplative an equally apt description? If you call yourself stupid, try changing that to life-long student.

Enjoy the challenge of stretching to understand how traits you viewed as liabilities might actually be assets in your children and yourself.

• Family dinners: making the connection

The National Center on Addiction and Substance Abuse (CASA) at Columbia University released its findings of a 2003 survey in a report entitled "CASA National Survey of American Attitudes on Substance Abuse VIII: Teens and Parents." The survey showed a correlation between frequent family dinners and reduced risk that teens would smoke, drink, or use illegal drugs. The results were consistent with other surveys conducted by CASA.

Teens who have dinner with their families two or fewer nights per week are at double the risk of substance abuse compared with teens who dine with their families more frequently. At the same time, family dinners drop off as teens move from middle school to and through high school. This decline occurs at a time when teens are at increased risk to abuse substances simply because of their age. Teens who eat dinner with their families five or more times per week report less stress, less boredom, and greater academic success.

This important and significant information is reporting a correlation, not a cause and effect. That means we cannot conclude that families who eat dinner together fewer than three times a week cause their children to abuse substances. However, families who eat dinner together five or more times each week reduce the risk that their teen will smoke, drink, or use illegal drugs.

You know all people are born with genetic needs that are experienced as an urge to behave. The most important of these is the urge for love and belonging. Each person desires the feeling of connectedness. Teenagers are no exception to this. However, developmentally, teenagers are also feeling an increased urge for freedom and independence. Teenagers are experimenting to discover new and different ways to feel powerful as well as connected to their newly emerging power group, their friends.

Despite what middle and high school children say, staying connected to their families is very important. This is not an either-or situation. Children want to feel the solid foundation of love, belonging, and connection to their parents at the same time they want increased freedom and connection with their friends.

Of course teenagers, driven by an increased need for power and freedom, hardly show or acknowledge their desire to remain connected to family. "Oh Mom, do I have to go to dinner at Grandma's? My friends and I had plans!" This type of complaint is often thrown at parents by their teen.

Children may also be increasingly involved in independent clubs, sports, and activities as well as plans to be with their friends. If one child has softball practice until five thirty in the evening while another has a meeting for his social studies project at a friend's house that begins at six thirty that same evening and the third has piano lessons squeezed in, how is it possible for a family to have an evening meal together? In addition, in many families both parents are working outside of the home with less time available to shop for and prepare an evening meal for the family.

But the information you know from the CASA survey and from peaceful parenting cannot be ignored. Families who eat together frequently are creating opportunities for all to meet their need for love and belonging with the family.

This solid foundation increases the likelihood that our children will have greater academic success, be less bored, less stressed, and less likely to get into trouble with cigarettes, drugs, and alcohol.

Work together as a family to make weekly plans for the nights you will all sit down together for dinner. Taking into account everyone's schedule, make a plan where everyone is taking some responsibility for making the meal and being at the meal together.

Perhaps eating dinner together five times a week will be the goal you all strive for. Maybe you won't make this target every week, but setting family dinners as a priority for the family gives your children the solid foundation they need for success.

Family dinners give you all the opportunity to connect with each other, to learn about each other's daily lives, and to discover the joys and challenges each person faces. Family dinners are a consistent practice that will help you all follow your genetic drive for love and belonging with each other.

No matter what your teenagers tell you now, family dinners will be a significant, positive part of their childhood now and their childhood memories in the future.

 Appendix C

Additional resources

Books

Buck, Nancy S. *Peaceful Parenting*. San Diego: Black Forest Press, 2000. Explains the application of choice theory to parenting in greater theoretical depth.

Dormer, Cindy. *Hold That Thought For Kids: Capturing Precious Memories through Fun Questions, Images, and Conversations*. Englewood, CO: BrightSide, 2004. This book guides you through an interactive scrapbooking type of process, helping you get to know your child while you track her progress.

Kohn, Alfie. *Punished by Rewards: The Trouble with Gold Stars, Incentive Plans, A's, Praise, and Other Bribes*. Boston: Houghton Mifflin, 1999.

Kohn, Alfie. *Unconditional Parenting: Moving from Rewards and Punishment to Love and Reason*. New York: Atria Books, 2005. Both books are worth reading. Although Kohn does not use a choice theory approach, the case he makes citing overwhelming research will convince you to move from an external approach to internal psychology.

Lipton, Bruce. *The Biology of Belief: Unleashing the Power of Consciousness, Matter and Miracles*. Santa Rosa: Mountain of Love/Elite Books, 2005. Explains the new science of molecular biology and its larger implications for personal relationships and life-long navigation.

Primason, Richard. *Choice Parenting*. New York: iUniverse, 2004. Another wonderful book using choice theory to guide parents.

Web Sites

Alfie Kohn, http://www.alfiekohn.org. Books, articles and much more about Alfie Kohn and his research and work.

Bruce Lipton, Ph.D., Uncovering the Biology of Belief, http://www.brucelipton.com. More information, articles and explanations about Dr. Lipton and cellular biology.

The Parenting Doctor, http://www.parentingdoctor.com. A useful Web site with lots of information and resources for parents of young children.

Peaceful Parenting Inc., http://www.peacefulparenting.com. More information about Dr. Buck, and parenting, as well its resources, and contact information.

The William Glasser Institute, http://www.wglasser.com. Learn more about choice theory, the psychological foundation for this book, as well as more resources and training.

Acknowledgments

My father, Floyd E. Smith, never met a person he couldn't teach. I'm happy to be one of those people. Dad recommended I read my first William Glasser book, *Reality Therapy*. That book set me off on the path I have followed all of my adult life. My journey has brought me to many parts of North and South America and Asia as well as Australia and New Zealand. Thank you, Dad.

I wish to acknowledge Dr. Glasser and all of the William Glasser Institute members throughout the world. Learning and teaching choice theory has been my mission. To all those people who came to listen, play, and grow with me, thank you. Please know that I was learning from you, too. People who study and apply choice theory hold a different vision of our relationships and of the world. Although it often feels like we are alone, together we are making a difference. I'm so grateful to have met each of you.

To the many people who supported my first book, *Peaceful Parenting*, thank you. To the many parents who have contacted me to let me know how this book has helped you, thank you. And to my business partner and big sister, Susan Martin, thank you for all the years of support, endorsement, and encouragement. I could not have done any of it without you. Plus it was more fun with you.

Thank you to Sharon Goldinger and all your staff at PeopleSpeak. You are the best bookmakers I know!

And finally I would like to acknowledge my family. How lucky I was to have my parents, although they are no longer on this earthly plane, who were my first fans and guides. Thank you to my two sisters, who joyfully continue to teach me to dance and play.

And with great pride I thank my two sons, who continue to teach me best about true love.

Index

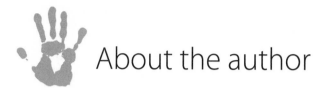# About the author

N ancy S. Buck, Ph.D., tackles the tough topics facing all families. She earned a doctorate in developmental psychology with an emphasis on parenting. Dr. Buck is the founder of Peaceful Parenting, Inc., which is based on her experiences as an educator, trainer, and above all, parent. For over two decades she has been a senior faculty member of the William Glasser Institute and has trained thousands of educators and other professionals in choice theory, reality therapy, and how to become a Glasser Quality School. Starting with her first book, *Peaceful Parenting*, she has been applying her knowledge and expertise to parenting. Her mission? To make the world a better place for all children and their parents.